The Kids' Book of
Incredibly
Fun Crafts

Illustrations by

Norma Jean Martin-Jourdenais

Roberta Gould

Library of Congress Cataloging-in-Publication Data

Gould, Roberta, 1946-
 The kids' book of incredibly fun crafts / Roberta Gould.
  p. cm.
 Includes index.
 Summary: Provides instructions for a variety of projects, including Ukranian dyed eggs, Mexican aluminum ornaments, and woven vine baskets and wreaths, using recyclable, natural, and easily available materials.
 ISBN 1-885593-85-6
 1. Handicraft--Juvenile literature. 2. Recycling (Waste, etc.)--Juvenile literature. [1. Handicraft.] I. Title: Incredibly Fun Crafts. II. Title.

TT160.G65 2003
745.5--dc21

                                          2003043092

Kids Can!® series editor: Susan Williamson
Project editor: Emily Stetson
Cover and interior design: Sarah Rakitin
Interior illustrations: Norma Jean Martin-Jourdenais
Photographs: Roberta Gould
Printing: Quebecor World

Williamson Publishing Co.
P.O. Box 185
Charlotte, VT 05445
(800) 234-8791

Printed in Canada

10 9 8 7 6 5 4 3 2

Kids Can!®, *Little Hands®*, *Kaleidoscope Kids®*, *Quick Starts for Kids!®*, and *Tales Alive!®* are registered trademarks of Williamson Publishing.
Good Times™ and *You Can Do It!™* are trademarks of Williamson Publishing.
Parts of this book were previously published in Roberta Gould's *Making Cool Crafts & Awesome Art*.

Notice: The information contained in this book is true, complete, and accurate to the best of our knowledge. All recommendations and suggestions are made without any guarantees on the part of the author or Williamson Publishing. The author and publisher disclaim all liability incurred in conjunction with the use of this information.

Dedication

For Stanley Robert Gould, 1919–1996, who had a very interesting life because he didn't understand the meaning of the word bored.

Keep Our Kids Safe!

As with all activities involving children, please be sure an adult is supervising. Set clear rules for using the stove, oven, a hot glue gun, an iron, sharp scissors, and other potentially dangerous tools. If younger children are present, please be certain that hot or sharp items are not near the edge of a table or countertop. Thank you.

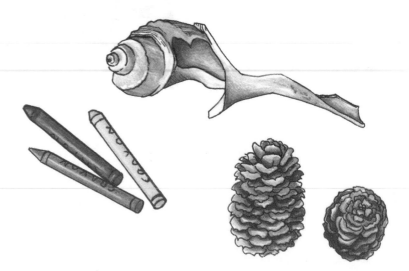

Acknowledgments

I want to thank all of these photogenic kids for their great ideas and wonderful creativity!

A's: Aaron Soriya Pen Kruger, Abigail Judith Naras, Abram Elias Escamillo, Acacia Quien, Adriana Michelle Avila, Aisha Khan, Ajay Kumar Rattan, Alan Gael Gallegos, Alana Trieschmann, Albert Buck-Bauer, Alice Reichman, Allison Cooper, Allison Heffley, Allison Menzimer, Amaya Blanco Ramirez, Amber Marion Bacon, Amy J. Mejia, Amy Rinaldi, Ana R. Ruano, Anahi, Andres Hamir Urena Hernandez, Angela Quiñonez, Annie Chin, Annie Pennell, Antoine L. Robinson, Anya Black, Anya Goldstein, Ari Usher, Arwen Thoman, Asa Kalama, Audrey Beil.

B's: B. B. Said, Ben Kalama, Ben Rudiak-Gould, Benjamin Derish-Luby, Benjamin Pennell, Bernadette McVerry, Bethany Lynn Woolman, Bianca Smith, Bill Holden-Stern, Breaunna Michelle Austin, Brenda Muñoz, Brigette Stump-Vernon, Brittany Terry.

C's: Caitlin Heffley, Caitlin, Camilla Santos, Carl Gould, Carlos I. Sempere C., Carmen Ruda, Caroline Thow, Carolyn Audrey Thompson, Carolyn Earnest, Carolyn Nguyen, Carrie Meldgin, Carrie Peterson, Casey Jackson, Chang Saechao, Charlie Buck-Bauer, Cheng Lai Saechao, Christian A. Cordova, Clare Nicole Kruger, Colin Burke, Colleen Smallfield, Cor Despota, Corey Spears, Cristy Peterson.

D's: DaMonica Mason, Daniel Goodman, Daniel Lawrence, Daniel Reichman, Darleen Ashlee Aragon, Daryl Shaun Myers Jr., Daveed Daniele Diggs, David Hackett, David Meldgin, Derrick L. Vassey, Dulce Hernandez, Dylon Felix Hasert.

E's: E. A. Grinstead, Eileen Beil, Eli Liebman, Elizabeth, Elizabeth Brokken, Elizabeth Prindle, Ellen Streit, Emily Black, Emily McKeown, Emily Walters, Emily Zubritsky, Emma Silvers, Estefania Padilla, Evonté L. Brown.

F's: Fernando Barela, Ferrari May Suiex Pharn, Fiona Gladstone, Fou Linh Saechao, Frances Perez, Francesca Danby.

G's: Gabe Scaglione, Genevieve Michel, Gina Saechao, Graham Guletz.

H's: Hannah Guletz, Hannah K. Moore, Hester Chambers Mills, Hilary Armstrong, Honey Bee Evans, Hugo.

I's: Iain Burke, Ieisha Kelly, Ilana Caplan, Isa Guardalabene.

J's: Jacob Delbridge, Jacob Hague, Jacob Winik, Jacquelyn Rohrer, Jake Niles, Jamie, Jamie Lincoff, Jarroue Holloway, Javier Santos Jr., Javontae Felix, Jazmin Uriarte Castro, Jed Loveday-Brown, Jeff Cooper, Jeffery Hartwell, Jenny Nungaray, Jesse Schumacher, Jesse V. Muñoz, Jessi Rodriquez, Jessica Areas, Jesus Javier Ayala, Jesus Robles Jr., Joanne Dolor, Jocelyn Davies, Jocelyn Romero, Joe Holden-Stern, John Casey Jones, Jonathan Ball, Jorge A. Trujillo, Jorge Alberto Barrientos, Joy Proctor, Juliana Pirkle.

K's: Kaela O'Brien, Kai Huntamer, Kaitlin Friedman, Kana Kobayashi, Karen Nakasato, Kari Gjerde, Karl Robinson, Karolyn Wyneken, Katherine Winkelstein-Duveneck, Katie Jensen, Keina Kiuchi, Kelly Tomacino, Keri Saechao, Kevin Gutierrez, Kimberly Mei Aller, Kiri Jones, Kory Sutherland, Krista Smith, Kyle Kemp.

L's: Lauren Finzer, Lauren Higley, Lauren Trieschmann, Leif Pipersky, Leon Traysean Small, Lily Ray Wyss, Lissette Alaniz, Lorain Pauline Garcia, Luis Alfredo Morales, Luke Tyler Hissom, Lyal Michel, Lucia Graves, Lydia Arce.

M's: Madeleine Whittle, Marcus Toriumi, Margarita Suarez, Marjorie Rose Gomez, Marshala A. R. Williams, Marta Blanchard, Marta Reyes, Marvin Escalante, Mary Ernie L. Navarro, Mary Nguyen, Max Green, Matthew Delbridge, Maya Dobjensky, Maya Sanchez-Haller, Meir Berman, Mercy Soto, Michael Clement, Michelle Kim, Michi, Mika Endo, Mira Bullen, Mirleni Vargas, Mitchell Green, Mitchell Karam, Miya Frank, Miya Kitahara, Mollie, Molly Anixt, Molly Gould, Molly Munch Di Grazia, Morgan B. Wilson, Moung Tong Saechao, Mykel Chamber/Barrett.

N's: Nariman Safizadeh, Natalie Buck-Bauer, Natalie Gonzales, Nathan Rynerson, Nathanael Larrabee, Nathaniel Rudiak-Gould, Nicholas Danby, Nicole Berger, Noah Raksmey Pen Kruger.

O's: Oliva Hernandez, Osa Jonmarker, Osiris Henderson.

P's: Pamela H. Ong, Parker Menzimer, Patrick Lawson, Paula Robinson, Peter Rudiak-Gould, Phoebe Wong, Pilar Aracely Hernandez.

R's: Rachael Masterson, Rachel Krow-Boniske, Rachel Schultz, Rachel Shoshana Berman, Raul De Leon, Raymundo Jimenez, Ricardo Ortega, Richard Michel, Rebecca Krow-Boniske, Robert Arthur Seares, Robin Anne Fink, Rom, Romana Ferretti, Roslind A. Woodard, Roxie C. Perkins, Ryan Mueller, Ryo Huntamer.

S's: Sabina Khan, Sam Blau, San On Saechao, Sapna Kumari Sharma, Sara Muse, Sara Schultz, Sarah Adams, Sarah Dobjensky, Sarah Leff, Sarah Rose Barrett, Sarah Streit, Sean Smith, Selena Ross, Shanidra Q. Brown, Shaquille Omar Page-Wilson, Shay Finnegan, Sherry Lee Aragon, Sierra Liebman (C.C.L.), Sierra Miley-Boland, Simone Woods, Solange LeRoux, Solomon Wong, Sophia Perkis, Sophie Linder, Sophie Weiss (C.C.), Sophie Winik, Spencer McNamara, Stefan Goldberg, Summer Jackson, Stephanie A. Romero, Stephanie L. Hernandez, Stephanie Magallan Montano, Stephanie Yien Fou Liew, Stephany Judith Naras, Stephen McKone, Steven TunLin Halverson, Sunny Nguyen.

T's: Takashi Israels, Tanzania Avington, Tara Mongkolpuet, Tavi Kessler, Teresa Montes, Tess, Tessa Jordan Breedlove, Tomisha Pickett, Travis Switzer, Tristan Chao.

V's: Vanessa Wellbery, Vivienne S. Carlsen.

W's: Walker Shapiro, Walter Pimentel Xavier, Waylon James Bacon, Wynona Marie Bucay.

Y's: Yadira Solis, Yoshi Smith.

Z's: Zach Walters, Zack Larson, Zenaida Hernandez, Zoe Ballance, Zoe Griffith, Zoe Steverson.

✳ CONTENTS ✳

INCREDIBLE FUN AHEAD!

First and foremost, this book of crafts is about the incredible person who will make them: YOU! You are unique, and therefore your crafts will be, too. Don't try to make your crafts look like any others, or to second-guess your creative impulses. Just go for it! Fire up your imagination, let your creative mind go to work, and start expressing yourself!

Use these ideas as a springboard for self-discovery. Don't worry about not having the exact tool or the precise kind of paint for a given project — use whatever you have on hand. Improvising adds spice to life, and who knows — maybe you'll figure out a better way of doing it! Feel free to change the projects, to cut them short, or to expand them. Each time, you'll undoubtedly come up with new ideas. That's what creativity is all about — looking at existing materials and methods and then building on them in ways that reflect you and your unique interests. As you improvise, you'll learn to throw away less and create more, to find new uses for things that aren't being used for their original purpose — to make something magical from something mundane!

You'll find you can make most of the crafts without any help. That's because in art there really is no "right" way to do something. And because there is only one of you, your crafts will look different and function in unique ways. Celebrate that individuality! Allow it to flourish! After all, the special dimension in making art is YOU!

✳ Make a Mess! ✳

Bet no one has ever said that before! But creativity and self-expression usually involve a workspace you can call your own. If you are lucky, you have a porch or yard where you can work without worrying about spilling stuff. Outside is a great place to work because the fresh air takes away some concerns about ventilation. Plus, you can be a bit noisy without bothering anyone, there's plenty of space to be creative, and it's easy to clean up. Ideally, there will be a space indoors, too, where you can work, but where you don't have to sweep the floor or apologize for the mess. Find a creative nook or corner where

1) there's good ventilation

2) you can safely leave your stuff out without putting everything away each time

3) you won't be ruining something — like a carpet or table — in the process.

When you set up a creative environment that fits you just right, you'll be surprised and delighted with the amazing things you can make!

✳ Free Stuff for Fun, Fun, Fun! ✳

Many of these crafts use materials that are found around your home, yard, or school. Best of all, most of the materials are free. You can save all sorts of potential craft materials — from recycled plastic milk jugs to broken electronic items — to have on hand when you make art. Having shelves of various art materials is a good idea, and it's also fun to have boxes of goodies for specific projects. You can put all the broken electronic odds and ends into a box, for instance, then do a project once you have a nice stash. Sort and organize the "junk," so you know what is there. It will get your ideas flowing. It's especially fun to set out five or 10 random items. Examine them, turn them over, and before you know it — bingo! — a creative idea will spring to mind. Soon, you'll begin to look at everything with the question: "How can I use that?" Well, just about anything is possible!

✳ Wait! Don't Throw That Away! ✳

Your family already may be doing a great job of minimizing the amount of packaging brought into your home by "wise shopping," but you may still be throwing away a lot of wonderful craft materials without even knowing it. That empty roll from the plastic tape is precious — it's a wheel for a car or a game piece. Those empty film canisters could be used to make toy binoculars and the lids used to make doll glasses. Do you have clothes with worn knees or elbows? Save the buttons and good fabric scraps. After you've used all the paper in your spiral notebook, keep the metal spiral and twist it into a useful sculpture.

Here are some items to have around if you want to be able to make almost anything. Don't worry if you don't have all of these things — this is just the start of your wish list!

Aluminum foil • beads • bottles (small ones from extracts or spices; large plastic jugs) and caps • boxes and cartons (all sizes and thicknesses) • broken toys and toy parts • cassette tapes (used, unneeded, taken apart) • cloth (from old clothes, sewing scraps) • corks • crayons • envelopes (used) • film canisters • hangers • leather and fake fur (from worn car-seat covers, coats, slippers) • magazines • nature finds (pinecones, twigs, rocks, vines, grasses) • packaging ("popcorn" pellets, bubble wrap, netting from veggies and fruit) • pantyhose (old) • paper (one side already printed) • paper clips • paper-towel and toilet-paper tubes • plastic containers and lids (all sizes) • plastic-foam trays (from fruits and veggies *only*; never from meats) • Popsicle sticks • ribbon, rope, string, and yarn • rubber bands • shells (only from very plentiful beaches; never with anything inside) • shoulder pads (from clothes) • stamps (used) • straws • stuffing (from pillows) • thread and tape spools • twist ties • wax (from cheese wrapping, old candle stubs) • wood scraps • wrapping paper

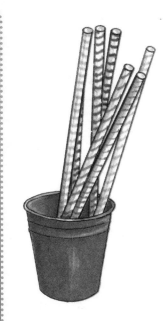

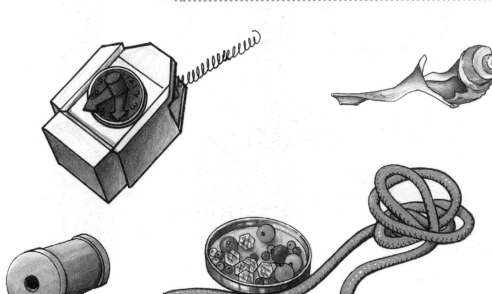

Incredible Fun Ahead!

✴ From the shelves or store ✴

Here are some things you may want to
collect or buy that you'll use over and over.

Awl*

Chalk

Clay, modeling or homemade (page 27)

Colored paper

Colored pens, markers, pencils, crayons

Drill (small, cordless)*

Food coloring

Glitter

Glue, glue sticks, glue gun*

Hammer, nails*

Knives (serrated)*

Needles, thread

Paint: acrylic, fabric, tempera

Paintbrushes

Permanent pens (use outdoors or in
    well-ventilated room)

Pins, safety pins

Scissors (strong, metal ones)*

Stapler

Tape: wide packaging, masking, and clear

Toothpicks

*Keep It Safe!, page 11

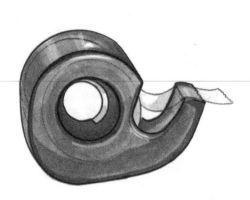

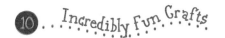

Keep It Safe!

Some of the projects in this book require tools that can be dangerous if used incorrectly. Always have an adult supervise you while working with knives, hammers, glue guns, awls, and any kitchen appliances. Follow house or school rules about supervision, and always keep younger children away.

Glue guns are wonderful tools, but require caution when using them. Ask an adult to help you find a place to set up the glue gun and to set it down when hot, and to check that you are using the glue gun correctly. Avoid touching the tip end, which can be very hot. Unplug when not using.

Sharp tools. Never work with sharp scissors, knives, awls, or a hammer and nails without an adult around. *Serrated knives* (the kinds with a saw-like edge) work great for cutting through hard materials, and their pointed ends are good for piercing cardboard and plastic. Always be sure you work on a flat, steady surface when cutting, and cut *away* from your body. Make sure no one is close by, in case the knife slips. *Awls* are particularly useful for poking holes in heavy cloth or leather; while a *hammer and nail* work well for making holes in metal. Keep all sharp or heavy tools away from the edge of the table or counter.

Drills can be dangerous … so ask an adult to help you use even a small cordless drill and to set up a safe workplace. Always wear protective glasses when drilling.

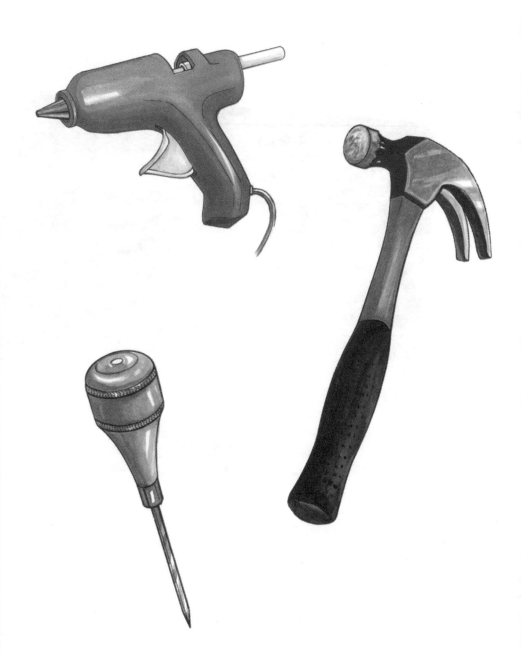

TAKE THE CHALLENGE!

All craft projects are labeled by various levels of challenge, just to give you some idea of what's involved. But you are talented enough to do any of them! So don't let a more difficult rating or suggested age/grade level keep you from any of these projects.

Level of Challenge: 1

If you are a second grader or older, you should be able to make these projects fairly easily. Younger kids may want some help from adults or siblings. A parent or teacher can easily use these projects with a classroom-size group.

Level of Challenge: 2

If you are in fourth grade, these projects will be fairly easy. Younger kids may benefit from help from friends and relatives. Adults working with groups of kids might want a few helpers.

Level of Challenge: 3

These projects are just a little bit harder and involved. Adults working with groups of younger kids may need several parents or older kids to help.

INCREDIBLY FUN CREATIONS!

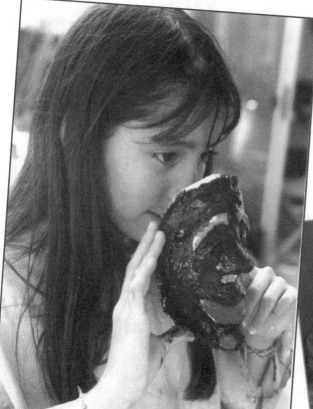

Celebrate your creativity as you play, laugh, and most of all, have fun! Make a flip book that tells a story, a robot with its own character, a claymation film that seems to have a life of its own, or totally awesome landscape cakes or countdown calendars that you design, construct, and then eat. You are unique and special, so ham it up and celebrate!

✳ Flip-Book Animation ✳

Create your own fast-action "story" with paper, pencil, your thumb, and your vivid imagination. Try sticking to a single idea that unfolds as your drawings progress; then, after you've drawn the main action on every page, you can go back and add more detail, background, and color.

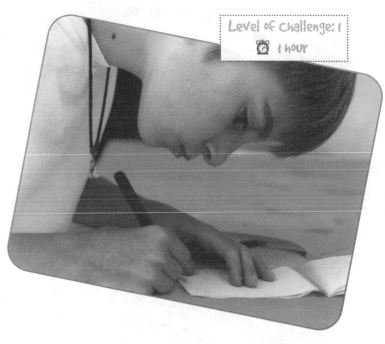

What You Need

✳ Small unlined notepads or self-stick notepads
✳ Pens, pencils, markers, crayons

What You Do

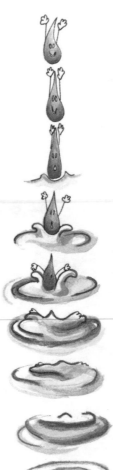

1. Think of an action that can be drawn as if it were in slow motion. It shouldn't need words to be clear (see ANIMATION IDEAS, right).

2. Draw a picture to start your action on the *last* page of the pad, near the bottom of the page. Go over the picture with dark lines so you can see it when you flip the page.

3. Go to the next-to-last page and, using your previous drawing as a guide, make a second drawing that continues the action. (Think of the progress of a cartoon.) Be sure the drawing isn't too different from the first, or the drawings will seem to skip around when you flip your book.

Animation ideas
✳ Balls bouncing and being thrown
✳ Drops of water falling and splashing
✳ A person walking, dancing, or doing jumping jacks
✳ A plant growing, blooming, and dying
✳ A skater spinning
✳ A horse galloping over a hurdle

4. Continue from the back forward, moving the action a little further along on each new page. Let the story unfold slowly. (It will seem fast when the book is flipped.)

5. Keep the action moving for about 20 pages, or until your "story" is done.

6. Now, flip through your book from back to front and watch the action!

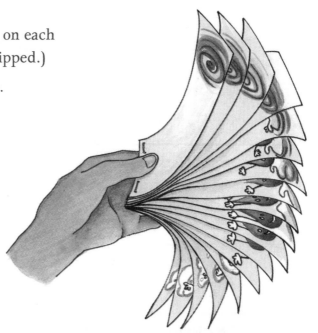

TAKING IT FURTHER

Cartoon Creations

Originally, animators had to redraw every scene when animating, just as you have done for your flip book. Today, it still takes many people to make the movement of all the characters you would see in a Disney movie. Full-length movies require as many as 65,000 pictures! (To try making your own *short* clay-mation film, see page 26.)

Computers now make the animation process much swifter, of course, and the new technology makes for some truly awesome animation. Watch some of the older car-toons, such as any of the *Looney Tunes* like Bugs Bunny (and the hapless Elmer Fudd) or Roadrunner. What differences do you notice between the animation in these cartoon classics and today's animated movies?

Japanese Anime (AH-nee-meh)

In Japan, animation isn't just for kids' fairy tales. It's used for a wide variety of audiences. The stories vary in style and quality, but some are very, very good. *My Neighbor Totoro* was dubbed over in English and released in movie theaters in the United States. It's a wonderful movie, but it's even better to see good anime in Japanese with subtitles. You can find it and others at an anime club or your local video store, or online at **<www.anime.com>**:

My Neighbor Totoro

Kiki's Delivery Service

The Castle of Cagliostro

Laputa: Castle in the Sky

Whisper of the Heart

✳ Countdown Calendars ✳

Caroline

Are you counting the days until a special event? Make the time go fast with a "countdown" calendar you design (and eat!). Count down the days until the winter solstice (page 42), Christmas, or to the beginning of Hanukkah, Kwanzaa, or the Chinese New Year. You can even count down the days until summer vacation! However you count it, this is just plain fun — and yummy, too!

Molding Fun

One of the most appealing things (besides the sweet treats themselves!) about making these calendars is that there are so many ways to create the molds. One year I had a bunch of individual jam containers, so my after-school art students glued them onto a backing and made the candy in them. Another year, we used egg cartons and covered the insides with microwavable plastic wrap. You'll probably invent other ways to make these molds, too. Just use what you have — it will be perfect! Then save the used plastic molds from the previous years' counting calendar and make new candies and covers for your next countdown.

WHAT YOU NEED

* Glue gun
* Plastic molds (from a previous year's store-bought candy calendar) or small containers (MOLDING FUN, left)
  * Cardboard
  * Candy chips, any flavor
  * Microwave*
  * Toothpicks
  * Stiff paper, pencil, ruler, scissors, and tape
* Markers, paints, crayons

Use only with adult supervision

Tiny Treasure Hunt

Fill the compartments behind the doors with non-candy treats — shells, beads, tiny toys (SMALL WORLDS, page 24), or even notes with a poem, a special thought, or an IOU that promises a finished chore!

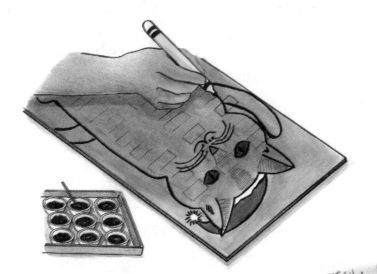

WHAT YOU DO

1. Glue the back of each plastic mold to a piece of cardboard that will fit in your microwave; let dry. If you are using egg cartons, line each depression with plastic wrap. If you have a readymade mold, skip to step 2.

2. Fill each depression with chips. Microwave the candy-filled mold for 1 to 2 minutes at half power (or on the "defrost" setting), or until the candies are soft enough to stir with a toothpick. (Since each microwave is different, check the candy every 30 seconds.) Stir all the compartments so that the candy is smooth.

3. Cut the paper so that it's about 2" (5 cm) larger than the mold on all sides. Place the paper on top of the mold. Mark a rectangular door for each compartment in pencil.

4. Remove the mold. Draw a beautiful picture on the front of the paper.

5. Cut three sides for each door, leaving one side attached. Label each flap with a different number.

6. Glue the back of the picture to the mold (be careful not to get glue on the candy!). Tape the edges of the paper over the ends of the mold. Then display your calendar, and count down with a sweet treat a day!

✳ Hexa-Flexagons ✳

You'll never know the meaning of the word *bored* once you try this mind-stretching puzzle! It's magic: You fold a long strip of paper in such a way that it appears to have only two faces, front and back, but when you flex it a certain way, you find another face — or as many as four more faces — that were hidden from view!

Ready to take the challenge?

What You Need

* Paper roll from adding machines or cash registers, or a 2 ¼"-wide (5.5 cm) strip of paper
* Scissors
* Pencil
* Glue
* Crayons, pens, colored pencils

Inventive Minds = Inventive Games

These cool puzzles were discovered by chance in 1939 when Arthur H. Stone, a young British math student, came to the United States to study at Princeton University. He brought his British binder along, but soon discovered that American paper was an inch (2.5 cm) too wide to fit. So Arthur made a quick fix and trimmed the paper, but ended up with a lot of long, thin paper pieces. Most people might have been tempted to just throw these extras away, but Arthur began to play with folding them in different ways — and in the process discovered these wonderfully perplexing shapes! He had so much fun with them that he showed his friends, and soon students and professors were folding and flexing and inventing even more kinds of flexagons!

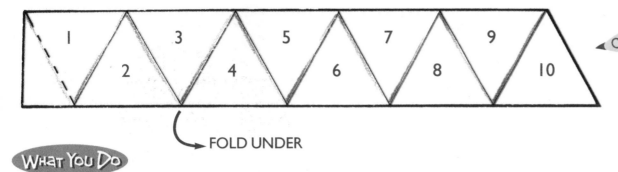

FOLD UNDER

Crafter's Clues

Easy Angle

To get the 60° angle, use a compass or make a cardboard equilateral triangle — each angle in any equilateral triangle is 60°. A triangle with three 2½" (6 cm) sides makes a good template that will give you just the right edge to trace.

What You Do

1. Cut a 15" (37.5 cm) strip off the paper roll. Cut one end at a 60° angle (EASY ANGLE, right). Now, make 10 equilateral (equal-sided) triangles on the paper strip by folding back and forth. Cut off the excess paper, and lightly label the strip with numbers in pencil (you'll erase them later).

2. Fold the long end of the strip *under* at the fold between triangles 3 and 4, so that the long end is pointing up.

3. Fold the top *under* at the arrows and place the end over triangle 1.

4. Fold triangle 10 *under* and glue it to back of triangle 1.

5. You now have a tri-hexa-flexagon with two "faces" (or sides), plus one hidden inside! Once you get the hang of flexing (page 20), decorate the three sides differently, and ask a friend to find the hidden side!

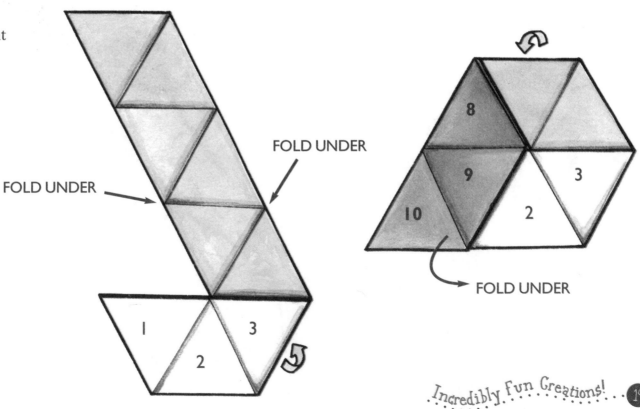

FOLD UNDER

FOLD UNDER

FOLD UNDER

Incredibly Fun Creations!

THE TRICK: THE FLEX!

The trick is to fold down in three places and push in on the other sides, forming three vertical folds. Then just open up the "flower" to find the hidden face. Keep folding and opening the folds until you get back to your original faces.

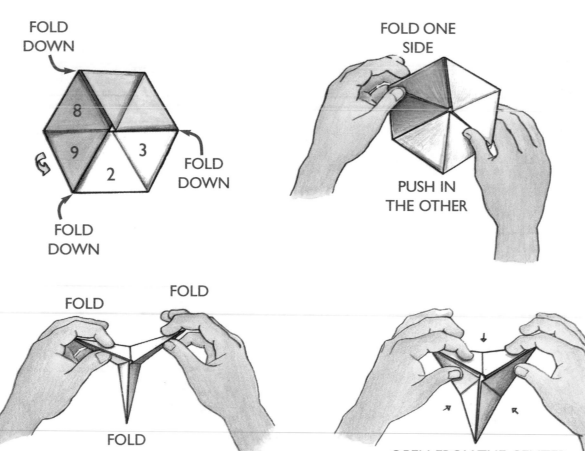

FOLD DOWN

FOLD DOWN

FOLD DOWN

FOLD ONE SIDE

PUSH IN THE OTHER

FOLD

FOLD

FOLD

OPEN FROM THE CENTER LIKE A FLOWER

NEW SIDE!

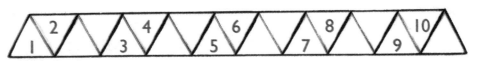

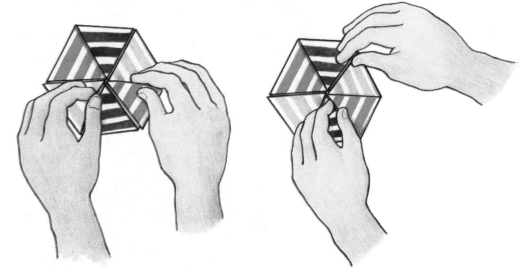

Hexa-Hexa-Flexagon
(six faces, *four* hidden!)

1. Cut a 30" (75 cm) paper strip, trim and fold it back and forth as for the hexa-flexagon (page 19), but this time make 19 equilateral triangles. Label it in pencil as shown (you'll have some blank spaces). Cut off the extra.

2. Now fold the strip at the heavy marks in a corkscrew manner, so that you end up with the numbers 1 to 10 showing side by side. Hold the folds together with clothespins or paper clips.

3. Fold this strip *exactly* as you folded the hexa-flexagon (page 19). Glue the flap next to 10 to the back of flap 1.

4. To flex, pinch and open the center as for the hexa-flexagon. There are four hidden faces, and finding them is a challenge — it may take you as long as an hour or as short as five minutes! When you find a new side, decorate it so you will recognize it when you come to it again.

Open Sesame!

If you can't open the hexa-hexa-flexagon when you pinch the three ridges, it means you've come to the end of that side. Pinch the three adjacent ridges and keep on flexing.

Funny Math

You might be surprised by how easy it is to find some of the sides — and how hard it is to find others! Here's a clue: Side 1 can be reached from sides 2, 3, 4, and 6. But side 6 can only be reached from sides 1 and 3!

TRY BOTH WAYS OF PINCHING

✳ Fabulous Fortune Tellers ✳

You don't have to have a crystal ball to tell a fortune! These fortune tellers are a blast to make (*you* get to decide on the fortunes!), and they're fun to play over and over. Make them as silly and far-fetched as you like — the more outrageous they are, the more fun!

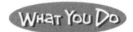

WHAT YOU NEED

* Square pieces of white paper
* Pencils, colored pens

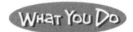

WHAT YOU DO

MAKING THE GAME

1. Fold the corners of the paper to the center; leave them folded.

2. Turn the paper over. Repeat the folding, using the new corners. You'll end up with four triangles.

3. Turn the paper back over and draw a different color on each square.

4. Turn to the back again and write the numbers 1 through 8 on the triangles, two for each folded section. Open out the triangles. Write a fortune for each number. Reclose all the flaps.

5. Turn back to the front. Put your fingers in the four flaps, pushing the corners down to make four points. You're ready to play!

Cooties, Anyone?

You're in good company if you like making fortune tellers — kids around the world have been making different versions of this game for ages. In Russia, they are called Gadalotschka; in Slovakia, Nebo Peklo; in Norway, Spå or Spålapp; in France, Cocotte en papier; and in the U.S. they are also called Cootie Catchers (referring, supposedly, to head lice!). You can call them whatever you want!

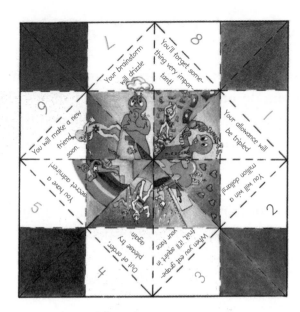

More Fortunate Fun

* Choose a theme. Give a fortune teller as a valentine. Fill it with compliments and good fortunes. Or make an April Fool's Day fortune teller, full of very silly fortunes.

* Make a fortune-teller party favor. Place the four points of your fortune teller facing down. The finger holds become four compartments for holding treats!

* Play the story-telling game Fortunately/Unfortunately, creating a hilarious story line by line with fortunate, then unfortunate scenarios, back and forth. The last player still telling the story, pessimist or optimist, is the winner.

* Watch the video, *That Man from Rio* as he goes back and forth from fortunate to unfortunate.

PLAYING THE GAME

1. Practice opening and closing the fortune teller, alternating front/back and sideways. Each time you open the fortune teller, you'll see only half the numbers.

2. Ask your friend to pick one of the four colors. Spell out the chosen color by opening sideways, then front/back, then sideways, and so on, saying a letter each time.

3. Your friend now looks inside and chooses one of the numbers. Count it out while opening and closing the fortune teller.

4. Ask your friend to choose one of the numbers shown on the inside flaps. Open up that number flap and read the fortune.

5. Now, show your friend how to make one so you can get your fortune told!

❋ Fortunate Ideas ❋

What fortunes can you think of? You can find examples on the Internet (search for "cootie catchers" or "fortune tellers"). Once you get going, you'll come up with lots of your own ideas! For more fun, customize the fortunes to the recipient!

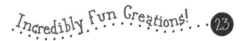

✳ Small Worlds ✳

Create your own small world — a place designed straight from your imagination, decorated with all kinds of things that are usually thrown away, ignored, or are considered by others to be "junk." Your small world can be a house of your dreams, with tiny homemade chairs, tables, beds, and sofas; a beach scene with shells, tiny driftwood, and sand; a forest retreat for fairies and gnomes, made of twigs, bark, pine needles, leaves, and acorn caps. Let your imagination run wild as you shape your own small world — you'll be amazed at all the ideas you come up with!

What You Do

Create, using small items to make common objects. Here are a few ideas for indoor decor from other kids to get you started. What can you use for a small world outdoors?

What You Need

* Knife (serrated or utility type)*
* Scissors
* Glue gun
* Lots of recycled materials and nature finds (WAIT! DON'T THROW THAT AWAY!, page 8)
*Use only with adult supervision

HOUSES

* Use a big flat box or package. Smaller cardboard boxes or plastic containers make one-room houses or different rooms.
* Cut out doors and windows so they open and close. Glue paper or self-sticking shelf paper to make wallpaper or wood walls. Old postage stamps make great paintings!

WINDOWS

* Glue a half of a clear cassette box to the wall of the house. Make an outdoor scene to fit behind it. Try different scenes for different times of the day or seasons!
* Add lace and cloth scrap curtains.

BEDS

* Make pretty pillows and bedding out of cloth and stuffing. (Shoulder pads make super pillows.)
* Use corks, cardboard, and foam to make bunk beds. Or make a tiny matchbox bed, Stuart Little style!

TABLES

* Use a thread spool, empty film container, or cork as the base. Make a round or rectangular top out of cardboard, plastic, or a metal lid. Some jam jar lids have a checkered pattern that is perfect for a tablecloth!

CHAIRS, STOOLS, SOFAS

* Use small yogurt containers, cutting out part for the seat. "Upholster" with foam and cloth.
* Make chairs, stools, and sofas with corks and craft sticks. What about a shoulder-pad sofa cushion?
* Use the wire cap that holds the cork on a champagne bottle to make a wonderful stool.

STORAGE

* Stack up empty matchboxes for a chest of drawers. Glue tiny beads on the front for door pulls.
* Cut cardboard for shelves. Hang them with triangular wall mountings underneath.
* Open out an individual (single serving) cereal box along the perforated lines. Decorate it inside and out to make a closet.

APPLIANCES

* Cut plastic foam to make sinks, refrigerators, stoves, washing machines, and toilets. Draw knobs and burners on the smooth surfaces with a permanent marker.

TAKING IT FURTHER

It's a Small, Small World

* Edible worlds. Make a small world you design and then eat! See Luscious Landscape Cake, page 30, and Magical Peek-In Sugar Eggs, page 82.

* Small peoples. Create a cast of small characters, using corks, twigs, fabric, yarn, straw — whatever you have on hand!

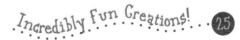

✳ Create a Claymation Film ✳

Ever wonder what goes on behind the scenes in movies? Make your own claymation movie and find out as you create a scene with toys, homemade playdough (page 27), and your fantastic imagination. Make a movie that tells a story you know. Or, just roll the video camera and see what develops, letting the story unfold as you go. Lights, camera, action — you're on!

What You Need

* Table
* White cloth or paper
* Lamps
* Video camera and tripod stand (if available)
* Masking tape
* Cardboard boxes, colored paper, glue, scissors, markers (optional)
* Props: small stuffed animals, blocks, boats, cars, dinosaurs, Legos, miniature people, trains, town pieces, alphabet letters, clothespins, pinecones, rocks, etc.
* Modeling clay or homemade playdough (recipe, page 27)

What You Do

SETTING THE SCENE

1. Cover the table with the white cloth or paper to reflect the light. Use lamps to light the scene.

2. Mount the video camera's viewing area securely on the tripod or other sturdy setup.

3. Center the camera on the table and focus on the area where your scene will be. Tape the edges of the area that the camera captures so you can keep the action in view. If you want, decorate a backdrop for your scene using a rectangular cardboard box with one long side cut out so the camera can see into it.

4. Now, plan your story and choose your props!

FILMING THE SHOTS

1. Set the first scene. Videotape about 4 seconds of the scene (this beginning helps your audience get ready for the action to come).

2. Begin changing the shape of the clay slowly, moving objects about $^1/_4$" (5 mm) per move. Press the ON button on and off as quickly as possible, once for each new position. More than one object can be moved each time, but try to keep the movement fairly simple. Make your animation as long as you want!

3. Gather your friends and family to watch your video on your TV.

Perfect Playdough

1. Mix 1 cup (250 ml) flour, ½ cup (125 ml) salt, and ½ teaspoon (2 ml) cream of tartar together.

2. Add 1 tablespoon (15 ml) vegetable oil and 1 cup (250 ml) water.

3. Cook the mixture, with adult supervision, over low heat, stirring continuously until it's thick. Remove from the heat.

4. Let the dough cool completely; then, knead it briefly.

5. Divide the dough into sections and add a couple of drops of different food colors to each section.

Super-Duper Scenes

* Combine playdough and objects; lumpy monsters swallow cars and buildings and then spit them out.

* Put wiggly eyes on playdough creatures; change creatures as you go.

* Let objects appear or disappear "magically" when you put them in or take them out of a scene.

* Create puzzles that put themselves together.

* Let block cities build themselves, fall, and rebuild.

Staying Focused

Keep your camera and your scene absolutely still; move only the action figures. Otherwise, you'll end up with a very jerky movie. Use clay or playdough to hold things in place, such as a car in a dinosaur's mouth or a tree on the side of a hill. Tie clear thread, fishing line, or even dental floss to objects so they look like they're flying, floating, or tilting.

✳ Robotology! ✳

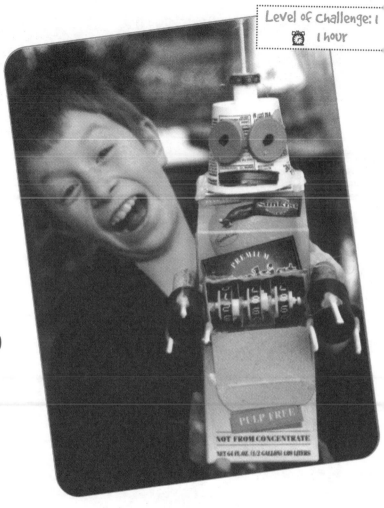

Think of all the different robots you have seen in movies or on television. Some of them are funny, some are cute, some are helpful, some are destructive — and some are really scary! Robots are used in real life to do many tasks, from making cars in factories to helping doctors perform surgery!

What kind of robot will you make?

What You Need

* ROBOT RECYCLABLES (page 29)
* Glue gun
* Masking tape or duct tape

What You Do

1. Rummage through your collected recyclables to find robot parts.

Body: A medium-size box, covered with aluminum foil.

Head: Look for packaging materials that seem to have eyes, a nose, or a mouth. Accentuate the features with other found materials. Add antennae, hair, and funny knobs.

Arms and legs: Your choice. Yogurt containers make sturdy legs and worn-out windshield wipers make excellent arms!

2. Glue and tape everything together so your robot will stand up.

Make It Real

* Use foil to cover plastic and cardboard pieces to make them look like metal.

* Attach wheels so your robot can move.

* Add an electronic control panel in the front, with glued-on buttons and knobs. Use corks, old parts from broken machines, bottle caps. Make a remote control.

Robot Recyclables

Look around your home, school, and outdoors — you probably have a lot of recyclable items you can use for your robot. Along with the typical list of trash treasures (page 9), look for broken and unfixable household machine parts or appliances, such as telephones, tape recorders, remote-control cars, old computers, disks, watches, calculators, radios, and old toys. Of course, ask permission first (*before disassembling!*), and *unplug all electrical appliances or machines* before touching them.

   Find a big box for your robot materials and label it ROBOT. Store your broken electronic things and robot-shaped packaging away in the box. Once your robot box is bulging with goodies, invite some friends over and let the excitement begin!

✳ Luscious Landscape Cake ✳

Did anyone ever tell you, "Don't play with your food!"? Well, here playing with food is required! Bake, design, decorate, and then eat a cake created to match your tastes. Devour a mountain or a city street, create a volcano snack or a lake with edible alligators … or even an edible computer!

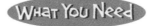

What You Need

* Cake batter (homemade or from cake mix)
* Cake pans, edged cookie sheets, metal cans
* Cardboard
* Aluminum foil
* Icing (page 32)
* Candies (page 32)

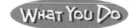

MAKING THE CAKE BASE

To make a big cake (say, for a whole party of kids), make six times a normal-size cake recipe. Use any flour cake recipes or cake mixes you like — the cake is just the raw material for creating the scene. Certain cake flavors are especially good for certain landscapes, though: Chocolate cake makes great mountains and volcanoes (Topo Tricks & Scene Savvy, page 31), strawberry and cherry cakes are good for southwestern scenes, and yellow cake with raspberry jam added looks like granite!

PUTTING IT ALL TOGETHER

1. Decide what you want your landscape to look like (Landscape Planning, page 31). Cover cardboard with aluminum foil to set your cake on.

2. Lay out your cake in the design you've chosen. Use icing wherever you will be putting candies and to smooth out the landscape. Skip the icing if you want the color of the cake to show.

3. Create a miniature world using various miniature candies. Set up little scenes in your big scene (page 32).

4. Serve the cake to your friends or family. They'll be glad to celebrate your creativity!

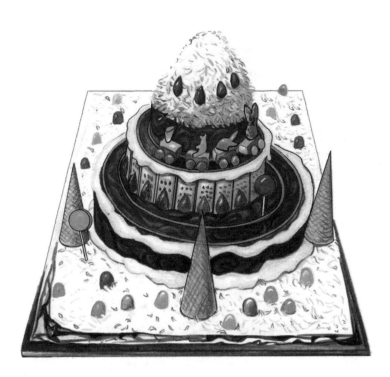

Topo Tricks & Scene Savvy

Layered mountains. Have you ever seen a topographical map? Each line on the map indicates a change in elevation. On the map, a mountain looks like a bull's-eye of concentric circles, but if you were there and wanted to get to the center of the circle, you would be hiking uphill! Well, a cake mountain is made with circles, too.

Bake the cake batter in edged cookie sheets. Cut a large piece of cake for the bottom layer (the base of the mountain). Cut each successive layer smaller so they look like a stack of large-to-small pancakes. Use a layer of icing between each layer of cake. Cover the cakes with icing to smooth the sides.

Round cake mountains, towers. Bake cake batter in tube cake pans. Or, pour cake batter into well-greased tin cans until they're half full, then bake. (Don't use very narrow cans, because the cake won't come out easily.) Use the whole cake as a mountain, or cut the cake in half to make tall cliffs.

Oceans and watery scenes. Use blue icing or blue gelatin for water. Make the gelatin on a large, flat cookie sheet (with sides) or other large pan, then transfer sections of hardened gelatin to the cake with a spatula. Make a smaller pond or a mountain pool by making gelatin in a clear bowl. Surround it with cake.

✳ Landscape Planning ✳

Local. Your house, your neighborhood, a park, a local farmers' market

Trips. Grand Canyon, a favorite lake or beach, summer camp

Maps. The world, the United States, Canada, your state

Imaginary. An imaginary world from a book, movie, or song

Favorite objects or pets. Computer, teddy bear, your St. Bernard!

Historical. Colonial village, Pompeii, your present-day hometown!

Ideal Icings

Basic Icing

This icing holds the cake layers together and makes a good foundation for decorations. To make, mix 1 package (8 oz/250 ml) softened cream cheese, 2 cups (500 ml) confectioners' sugar, and 1 teaspoon (5 ml) vanilla together until creamy and smooth. Add food coloring to dye the icing different colors.

Amazing Microwave Icing

Makes a huge amount of fluffy, moldable frosting to cover anything! Use powdered egg whites (available at grocery stores) rather than fresh eggs.

1. Stir together 2 cups (500 ml) sugar, ½ teaspoon (2 ml) cream of tartar, and 1 cup (250 ml) water in a microwave-safe measuring cup or bowl. Microwave* for 3 to 5 minutes, until the mixture boils.

2. In a large bowl, beat 4 tablespoons (50 ml) of powdered egg whites in ½ cup (125 ml) water until the whites form soft peaks (that means the egg whites hold their shape but are not dry and stiff).

3. With adult help, hold the measuring cup with a hot pad and pour the hot mixture slowly over the beaten egg whites while beating at medium speed. Then beat the mixture for several minutes at high speed.

4. Add the flavorings and colorings.

*Use only with adult supervision

Candy Characters & Treat Streets

* Gummy bear folks
* Chocolate cars and buses
* Good 'n' Plenty hot dogs
* Rock candy on a stick for streetlights
* Spearmint leaf trees
* Thin black licorice rope railroad tracks
* Jelly bean rocks, cobblestones, paths, eggs
* Caramel square bricks
* Shredded coconut (dyed with food coloring) grass, water, dirt, or snow
* Graham cracker walls and roofs
* Tootsie Rolls shaped into almost anything (warm them in the microwave*)

*Use only with adult supervision

✳ Marvelous Masks ✳

Do you love to be silly sometimes, experimenting with a new identity? It's a chance to be something you would never *dare* to be in real life, or to "try on" an identity you might like to be. Either way, it's loads of fun!

The easiest way to change your identity, of course, is by wearing a mask — it hides your unique, recognizable, smiling face! The transformation is immediate: When you put on a mask, you take on the characteristics of that mask, becoming wilder, more suave, sillier, ultraserious, smart-alecky, thoughtful, scared, brave, babyish, or domineering.

Explore your creativity of the moment as you make a fanciful mask, then change who you are for an hour or two!

LIFE MASKS OF PLASTER

Here's a mask you can make to fit your face exactly. In fact, no one else will be able to wear your mask — it's skin tight! Make it look as much or as little like your own face as you choose.

WHAT YOU NEED

* Headbands, scrunchies, hair clips
* Old shirts or clothes
* Petroleum jelly
* Mirror
* A partner!
* Fast-setting plaster bandage material (from a medical supply store)
* Scissors
* Lukewarm water, in a bowl
* Newspaper
* Hair dryer (optional)

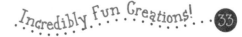

What You Do

Forming the mask

1. Pull all of your hair away from your face, and protect your clothes with an old shirt. You'll get very messy!

2. Cover your face *thoroughly* with a thin layer of petroleum jelly, using a mirror so you're sure to get all the spots. Be sure you include your eyebrows, up to the hairline on your forehead, under your chin, and on your eyelids, lips, and nostrils. Ask your partner to make sure you haven't missed a spot. This is important!

3. While you're getting covered, your partner cuts the bandage material into 1/2" x 3" (1 x 7.5 cm) strips.

4. Have your partner moisten one strip at a time in lukewarm water, rubbing the strip a little to moisten the plaster, then apply it to your face. Smooth each strip against your skin. Leave your eyes, nose, and mouth uncovered at the beginning so you're more comfortable.

5. Cover under your chin toward the neck. Decide if you want to close your eyes, mouth, and nose and have them covered. (But leave a space for breathing!)

Mask Magic

In theater all over the world, masks transform the identities of people, often from one gender to the other! In Africa, traditional masks were made to express nature in all its wildness and exuberance. Many American Indians made masks to represent animals and spirits. The Iroquois, of what is now New York State, carved scary, twisted, human-shaped masks in living trees to scare away the evil spirits they believed caused sickness.

If you're a little nervous about putting something on your face that will turn rock hard, that's understandable! Maybe you have a friend who is more comfortable with the process who can go first. You help him or her with the mask and then decide if you feel comfortable having one made on your face. You can also make a partial mask and cover only your chin, cheeks, and lips, or half of your face like the Phantom of the Opera!

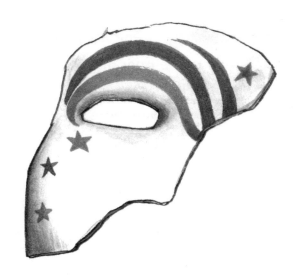

6. Have your partner crisscross the strips and apply several layers until the mask feels strong. Let the mask harden on your face for 5 to 8 minutes.

7. When hardened, lean forward, holding the mask in your hands, and make lots of facial expressions (scrunch face, wrinkle forehead, frown) to make the mask come off.

8. Place the mask carefully on a bed of wadded newspaper so it can finish hardening in the proper shape.

Crafter's Clues

Damp Dry

If the weather is cool or damp, use a hair dryer to dry the mask while it's on your face and after removing it. Otherwise, it may not harden properly.

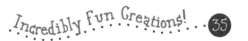

Facial Fun!

1. Add to the front of the mask (make a bigger chin, add warts, longer nose) with more strips of plaster bandage. Just don't make any changes to the inside of the mask, or it won't fit.

2. Let the mask dry for at least 30 minutes.

3. Paint if you wish.

4. Glue on feathers, shells, sequins, glitter, rocks, seeds, eyes, ribbons, yarn, or whatever else inspires you.

Feel the Heat

You may be asking yourself, "How does plaster harden and why does it heat up as it hardens?" It's all because of a chemical reaction. The chemicals in plaster stay separate until they are dissolved in water. But once dissolved, they react with each other and change chemically to a form that has less energy. The extra energy is released in the form of heat — which you feel as the mask hardens.

Mistaken Identity

You've probably read books or seen movies where the characters go to a masked ball to spy on or trick other characters in the story. Authors have thought of some wonderful plot twists involving mistaken identities. Watch a live production of William Shakespeare's *A Comedy of Errors,* or rent the movie *The Pink Panther,* to see how people use masks to disguise themselves. Can you trick anyone you know by wearing your mask?

MASQUERADE FEATHER-WORK MASKS

Elaborate feather masks are worn on Mardi Gras in New Orleans. The city comes alive with exuberant parades of costumed revelers, and wild dancing in the streets. Mardi Gras is a French word meaning "Fat Tuesday." This wild party is part of the culture in other countries, too, such as Brazil, Italy, France, and Germany, and is held at the beginning of March, at the end of the month-long Carnival celebration.

The idea of a wild winter party is much older than the first Mardi Gras, though. The ancient Babylonians celebrated the time between the fall harvest and the coming of spring with elaborate festivities. They even let masters and slaves exchange places temporarily. A similar tradition is still carried out today in Italy during Carnival, when families allow the children to be in charge and make the parents follow the rules!

What You Need

* Tracing paper, pencil, scissors, cardboard
* Glue
* Utility knife* or small, pointed scissors
* Feathers (from a craft store or old feather duster)
* Rubber band, yarn or string, craft stick
  Use only with adult supervision

What You Do

1. Make up a mask shape on tracing paper and trace it onto the cardboard. Cut it out. If the cardboard is thin, glue two layers together.

2. Ask an adult to help you cut out eyeholes with the utility knife or sharp scissors.

3. Glue feathers on the mask.

4. Add ties or a handle.

Adding Pizzazz

Layered Look

For a thickly covered feather mask, glue a first layer of small feathers around the outside of the mask, gluing just the quill end and letting the feathery end extend beyond the cardboard. Cover the quill ends with the next layer of feathers. Continue adding feathers, ending with small feathers around the eyes.

Crafter's Clues

Magnificent Masks

✦ Put extra glue around the eyeholes and sprinkle glitter or place sequins around the eye openings to cover up the last quills that show. Or, encircle the eyes with ribbons ½" (1 cm) wide, lace, or pretty shoelaces.

✦ Punch a hole in each side. Use a rubber band, string, or yarn to tie on the mask. Or, glue a craft stick handle on the center of the mask or off to the side, like opera glasses.

CREATING WITH LIGHT & SOUND

Usually when we think of creating art, hands-on materials like paper and paint come to mind. But you can create amazing art with light and sound, too! Discover how as you map the sky in dots of light, create a twinkling lantern, dip and mold candles of your own design, add a new twist to traditional candleholders, and record sound effects of the world around you!

✳ Light Designs from Tin-Can Lanterns ✳

Level of challenge: 2
⏰ 45 minutes, plus
1 day freezing time

The art of making something magical out of something mundane shines through (literally!) in this incredible craft. Transform a can destined for the recycling bin into a lantern that lets out sparkles of light in a one-of-a-kind punched-tin pattern designed by you!

What You Need

* Smooth-sided cans (from condensed milk, mandarin oranges), with top removed
* Permanent marker
* Water
* Cloth or towel
* Hammer and nails (several sizes)
* Wire (recycled handles from take-out food containers, or any flexible wire)
* Plastic lids, about 1" (2.5 cm) in diameter
* Glue gun
* Candle stubs
* Matches*

*Use only with adult supervision

What You Do

DAY 1

1. Plan your pattern, then mark it onto the side of the can with the permanent marker.

2. Fill the can with water to ½" (1 cm) from the top. Freeze solid (the freezing time will depend on the size of the can).

DAY 2

1. Wrap the cloth or towel partway around the can of ice. This insulating layer will help you hold the can without freezing your hands and will keep the can from rolling away as you hammer. Nail completely through the metal, making holes that match your pattern. Work quickly, so the ice doesn't melt.

2. Hammer two holes near the top of the can for handle attachments.

3. Let the ice melt. Bend the wire to form a handle through the two top holes.

4. Glue a plastic lid into the bottom of the can. Drip wax in the lid to secure the candle. Now light your lantern and enjoy the magic of your unique pattern of sparkling light!

Holes of Light

The more holes your design has, the more striking the effect. More holes also mean a brighter lantern. When hammering the design, choose nails of several sizes to get different hole sizes.

Large Lights

Try making a bigger lantern using a larger can. You can even make a gigantic lantern using a syrup tin can or an olive oil container!

✳ Winter Solstice Starry Sky ✳

On the darkest day of the year, celebrate the light! Sound crazy? Well, not really. In the Northern Hemisphere, the winter solstice — around December 21 — is the shortest day of the year, with the fewest hours of daylight. Since ancient times, people have celebrated this day, because it means the hours of sun will gradually increase. That extra daylight means spring days and sunny summer warmth are just a few months away!

There's another reason to celebrate the shortest day, too: During the longest night, you can get to know the starry sky! On a dark night, explore the constellations by making your own sky chart.

What You Need

* Flashlight covered with red plastic wrap
* Sky chart of the constellations, or a knowledgeable friend
* Black plastic-foam tray from store-bought mushrooms or vegetables, rinsed off
* Wooden skewer sticks or sharpened pencils

What You Do

1. On a clear winter night, go outside where you can see the night sky, away from street lamps and house lights. Wear plenty of warm clothes and make yourself comfortable on a reclining chair or a waterproof ground sheet (it's a lot easier on your neck that way!). Take a star chart with you, and a flashlight covered with red plastic wrap. This gives you enough light to read the chart, but still lets you easily see the stars. On a good night you can see as many as 3,000 stars in the sky, without binoculars or a telescope. Look for the huge celestial stream in the sky called the Milky Way, and for shooting stars, too!

2. See if you can pick out some of the main constellations (STARRY, STARRY NIGHT, right). And, while you're at it, make up a few of your own, searching the sky for patterns or shapes. Give them a name and make up a story about them, just as the ancient Greeks did!

3. Back inside, pierce the plastic-foam tray with your skewer or pencil to form the design of your favorite constellations. Hold your constellation up to the light, or shine a flashlight through the holes to project your pattern onto the wall.

THE WINTER SKY

N

Draco

Big Dipper

Little Dipper

Cepheus

Cygnus

Cassiopeia

Andromeda

Perseus

Pegasus

Gemini

Cancer

Aries

E

Pisces

Hydra

Taurus

Canis Minor

Cetus

Aquarius

Orion

Canis Major

Eridanus

W

S

Starry, Starry Night

One of the easiest constellations to find in the Northern Hemisphere during winter is Orion (oh-RYE-un). His three-star belt gives him away. See if you can find his raised club and his lion-skin shield.

To Orion's right is Aldebaran (al-DE-bah-ron), the brightest star in the constellation Taurus (the Bull).

In the other direction from Orion's belt is Sirius, the sky's brightest star, located in the constellation known as Canis Major, or the Big Dog.

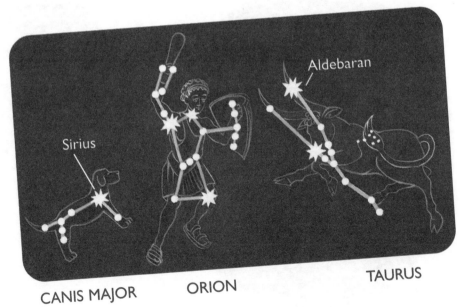

Aldebaran

Sirius

CANIS MAJOR

ORION

TAURUS

Other constellations to look for are Gemini, made up of the twins Castor and Pollux, which look like two stick figures holding hands. Cassiopeia, the queen lounging in her chair, looks like a big W in the sky. And, the most well-known constellation of all, the Big Dipper (also called the Great Bear) is also visible in winter. Once you've found the Big Dipper, look for the Little Dipper, and the bright North Star, Polaris, at the end of its handle.

The part of the Milky Way galaxy (the enormous spiral in space that includes our solar system) that we see from earth has been described as a stream, a trail of straw, a ribbon of smoke from a campfire, or — as the Pawnee Indians of the central U.S. describe it — a cloud of dust kicked up by the buffalo galloping across the sky. Other cultures think of the Milky Way as the road traveled by the dead, on their way to an afterlife in the heavens. Whatever you imagine it to be, this band of stars, planets, gas, and dust is truly beautiful to see!

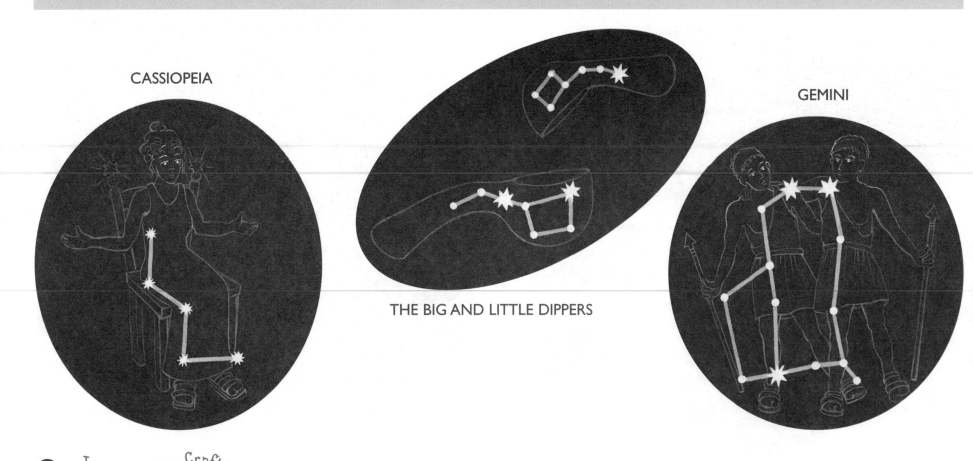

CASSIOPEIA

THE BIG AND LITTLE DIPPERS

GEMINI

Incredibly Fun Crafts

✳ Incredible Candles ✳

Celebrate the time-honored craft of making candles with some awesome new twists! Candle-making used to be a traditional fall activity, in which animal fat was rendered into tallow and then made into candles that would add light to the dark of winter. Today, many candles are made from a combination of beeswax and paraffin, a white wax made from petroleum, wood, and coal. You can experience part of the old traditions as you mold wax into unique candles that reflect your incredible creativity and imagination!

MOLDED CANDLES

Make simple candles from different colors of wax for whatever look you like. Try a simple layered design for starters; include flowers, shells, or other nature finds for a theme candle; mold a smooth egg-shaped candle from (what else?) an egg! Or make a one-of-a-kind candle with ice!

Layered Candles

What You Need

* Paraffin, beeswax, or recycled candle wax*
* 6 to 10 cans, for holding melted wax
* Large pot, for water bath
* Stove or hot plate, to melt wax*
* Food-warming tray (optional)*
* Hot pads and mitts
* Crayon stubs, for coloring wax
* Sticks, straws, or knitting needles, to stir wax and hold wicking
* Wicking (Wick Tips, page 47)
* Paper cups
* Scissors
* Old measuring cups, with pour spout (optional)

Use only with adult supervision

A Word on Wax

Wax melts at a fairly low temperature and is easily molded and colored, making it a wonderful medium to work with. Set the project up outdoors so you won't have to worry about the mess, and take the freedom to experiment!

Paraffin can be purchased at craft or grocery stores in slabs or blocks. You can also use *recycled wax* from candle stubs by melting the stubs and removing the wicks. *Beeswax* is a creamy yellow color and has a wonderful smell. It is expensive to buy, but even a small amount of it will give a natural scent to your candles. A local beekeeper may be able to give you some wax if you ask.

When working with any wax, *be extra cautious, and work only with adult supervision. Wax is dangerous when overheated. It should be warmed in a hot-water bath, never melted directly in a pan on the stove.* To make your own water bath, fill a large pot with 1" (2.5 cm) of water. Place a metal rack in the bottom to set the cans of wax on and heat the water. *Melted wax is very hot; keep it away from table edges, and well out of reach of young children.*

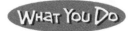

PREPARING THE WAX

1. Break the wax into pieces. Fill the cans about half full of wax.

2. Place cans in the water bath (A WORD ON WAX, page 46) on the stove or hot plate. With adult supervision, heat on low or medium until the wax is melted. Do not overheat! Turn off the heat.

3. Place cans on warming tray or keep extra wax melted by leaving it in the water bath, with the stove off.

4. Add crayons of your desired colors to the cans of melted wax. Stir thoroughly.

MAKING THE WICK

1. Twist the end of the wick around the middle of the stick, then place the stick across the top of the paper-cup mold, centering the wick.

2. Trim the wick so it almost touches the bottom of the mold.

MAKING THE CANDLE

1. Transfer a small amount of hot wax from one can to a drink or measuring cup so that it's easier to pour.

2. Pour your first wax color into the paper-cup mold to a depth of about 1" (2.5 cm). This will be the base of your candle. Let the wax cool about 10 minutes, until the surface is hard enough to support the next layer.

3. Repeat with the next color of wax. Continue on until you have three to five layers.

4. Let the candle dry completely — 30 minutes or more. Then tear and peel the cup away from the hardened wax.

5. Trim the wick to ¹/₂" (1 cm) and light your candle!

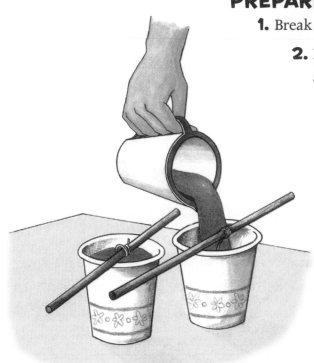

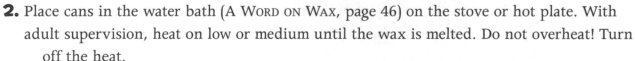

Crafter's Clues

Wick Tips

Wicking is the part of the candle you light. Wire-stiffened wicking is easy to use. You can buy it at a craft store or save wicks from recycled candles. (When you melt old candles, the wicks will fall to the bottom of the pan.)

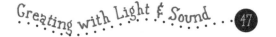

Seashell Candles

1. Make a plain molded candle in a 5 oz (150 ml) paper cup, following the directions for the LAYERED CANDLES (pages 46–47) but using only one color of wax, rather than layering.

2. When the wax has hardened, peel off the paper and place the small candle in a larger (8 oz/250 ml) paper cup. Fill around the edges with shells or bits of broken shells, facing the pretty side of the shells out.

3. Pour in more melted wax. Add more shells if necessary as you fill up the sides.

4. Cool 20 minutes and peel off the paper cup. Scrape off any wax covering the outside of the shells so you can see the patterns.

Flowery Candles

1. Make a plain molded candle in a paper cup, following the directions for the LAYERED CANDLES (pages 46–47), but using only one color of wax, rather than layering.

2. Let the wax harden, then peel off the paper cup and glue flower petals, small leaves, or other flat nature finds onto the candle's sides.

Eggshell Candles

An old-fashioned egg cup makes a fun candlestick for this egg-shaped candle!

What You Need

* Same supplies as for LAYERED CANDLES, page 46, plus:
* Eggs
* Safety pin or push pin
* Egg cartons

What You Do

1. Make a ¹/₂" to 1" (1 to 2.5 cm) hole in the *pointed* end of the egg using the safety pin. Don't poke a hole in the other end, or the melted wax will flow out the bottom!

2. Gently shake the insides of the egg out of the hole (refrigerate for scrambled eggs later!). Rinse the shell carefully, and wash your hands with soap and water.

3. Place the egg upright in the egg carton, with the hole at the top. Prepare the wax (page 47) and color it as desired. Center the wick in the egg, then fill around it with melted wax, or with layers of melted wax.

4. Let the wax cool completely, about 30 minutes. Peel off the shell and trim the wick.

Ice Candles

Wax and ice don't seem to be compatible, but together they make an amazing candle pattern!

* Same supplies as for LAYERED CANDLES, page 46, plus:
* Molds: Cardboard milk cartons (various sizes), salt, oatmeal, or potato chip containers
* Candle stubs, rather than wicking material
* Ice cubes or chunks, in sturdy plastic bag
* Hammer

Two-Toned Design

For a two-colored candle, don't make the last solid layer of wax on the top. Pour off the water when the wax has hardened, and pour another color of wax to fill up the spaces left by the ice and to make the solid layer on top. Remove the carton when the new wax hardens.

What You Do

1. Prepare the wax (page 47) and color as desired. Keep warm.

2. Cut the top off the cardboard mold and trim it an inch (2.5 cm) taller than your candle stub.

3. Smash bagged ice cubes or chunks with the hammer (do this outside!) into about ¹/₂" (1 cm) pieces. Don't make the pieces too small.

4. Fill the mold with ice to an inch (2.5 cm) of the top. Don't cram the ice in — you need to leave spaces for the wax. Place your candle stub, wick end down, into the mold so that the bottom is level with the top of the ice.

5. Pour the melted wax over the ice to the top of the mold. Let harden.

6. When the wax is cool, pour out the water and peel off the carton. You should see an intricate pattern of wax with holes where the ice was! Turn the candle over so the wick end is up. As the candle burns, it will show off the labyrinth pattern of the wax.

DIPPED CANDLES

Combine old ways of candle-making with some cool ideas of today! Experiment with this traditional form to see what you come up with.

Traditional Dips

What You Need

* Use the same supplies as for LAYERED CANDLES, page 46, except find the tallest cans you can to melt the wax (skinny olive oil cans are great). The candles will only be as tall as the depth of the wax.

What You Do

1. Prepare the wax (page 47) in the tall cans and color as desired. Keep warm.

2. Dip wicking or string in melted wax; remove. Air-dry for about one minute.

3. Dip again in the same color of wax and remove quickly. If you leave the candle in the melted wax too long it will remelt the previous layers and the candle will get thinner! Repeat until your candle is the desired thickness.

4. Trim the bottom of the candle so it's flat and hang by the wick end on a string until totally cooled. The candles will slump or bend if stood on their bottom or laid flat.

Crafter's Clues

No Water Added

Some dipped candle directions say to dip in wax and then dip in water. Don't do it! Pockets of water may develop between the layers of wax. When the candle is lit, the flame sputters and goes out!

Water Balloon Candle

* Same supplies as for LAYERED CANDLES, page 46, except use large round cans (such as large cookie tins) that are at least 8" (20 cm) in diameter and 5" (12.5) deep for the melted wax
* Water balloon
* Short candle

WHAT YOU DO

1. Prepare the wax (page 47) in the large cans and color as desired. Keep warm.

2. Fill the balloon with water until it is about 5" (12.5 cm) in diameter; tie securely.

3. Dip into the wax. Air-dry for a minute. Then repeat dipping 10 to 20 times, until a strong wax layer is formed.

4. Cool for 2 minutes, then pop the balloon by cutting the knot. Watch out for a fun fountain of water!

5. Pour a puddle of hot wax in the bottom and place a short candle stub inside for lighting.

Note: Keep all balloons and balloon pieces away from pets and small children to prevent choking hazard.

Candle Carvings

Carefully cut designs in the sides of the candle using a warmed kitchen knife (run knife under hot water and use only with adult supervision, please). Make a wax Jack-o'-lantern, and watch it glow when you light the candle inside!

✴ Craft a Candleholder ✴

During December, people of many different beliefs use candles or lights as part of their holiday rituals to brighten the darkness of winter. Take part in the customs of others by making candleholders that celebrate different traditions!

HANUKKAH MENORAH

Hanukkah, The Festival of Lights, is a 2,000-year-old celebration that starts on the 25th day of Kislev of the Jewish calendar, which corresponds to a day in late November or in December of our current calendar. Hanukkah commemorates the homecoming of the Jewish people and the miracle of the oil during the rededication of the Temple of Jerusalem in 165 B.C. As the story is told, the special oil that was meant to light the Menorah lamp for only one day lasted for eight days. To celebrate this amazing event, Jewish people light a special menorah with nine branches (candle holders) — one candle for each of the eight days and a "servant" candle, the Shamash, that is used to light the others.

Special Hanukkah candles are available at most grocery stores, but for this homemade menorah you can use birthday candles.

What You Need

* Round cardboard container with metal bottom (the type coffee, cocoa, or tea come in)
* Hammer and nail
* 9 birthday candles and 8 holders
* Lid from used water or squirt bottle
* Glue gun or modeling clay
* Permanent pens
* Matches*

Use only with adult supervision

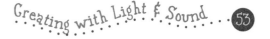

WHAT YOU DO

1. Peel off the paper label on the container to reveal the aluminum foil covering the cardboard. Turn the container over and hammer eight holes in a semicircle around the bottom edge. Leave room for the larger Shamash candle.

2. Glue or stick the eight candleholders into the holes. Insert the candles.

3. Glue the used lid in place. Insert the Shamash candle.

4. Decorate the silvery sides of the container. You might want to use some traditional Jewish designs such as the six-sided Star of David (page 11).

5. Use a match to light the Shamash, then use the Shamash to light the other candles. During Hanukkah, one candle plus the Shamash is lit the first day, two the second day, three on the third day, and so on until the eighth day, when all nine candles are lit. Traditionally, the candles are left to burn all the way out each day, but with your birthday candle menorah, you will need to blow out the candles before they burn down to the plastic holders.

TAKING IT FURTHER

Hanukkah Traditions

During Hanukkah, the family spends time together singing, reciting traditional Hebrew prayers, eating latkes (potato pancakes), and playing dreidel. Ask some of your Jewish friends to teach you some of their Hanukkah traditions.

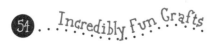

KWANZAA KINARA

Level of Challenge: 1

⏰ 1 hour to make

Kwanzaa is a fairly new holiday that is based on old traditions. It starts on the day after Christmas and ends on New Year's Day. Each of the seven days of Kwanzaa celebrates a certain value that affirms the good, strong qualities of the African American community.

You can celebrate, too, by making your own Kwanzaa Kinara!

WHAT YOU DO

You make a Kwanzaa kinara the same way you make the Hanukkah menorah (page 53), but with two fewer candles. Instead of four candles on each side of the center candle, you need only three. Traditionally, the tall candle in the middle is black, the three to the left are red, and the three to the right are green. The kinara itself symbolizes the roots of all African Americans.

During the first night of Kwanzaa, the black candle is lit; then the black candle and the red candle next to it on the second night; and the black, red, and green center candles on the third night; followed by the black, red, green, and another red candle the fourth night. You continue the pattern, lighting the preceding candles and another red or green candle each night. Each day is dedicated to thinking about a different one of the seven values, or *Nguzo Saba:* Unity or *umoja* on the first day, self-determination or *kujichagulia* on the second, collective work and responsibility (*ujima*) on the third, cooperative economics (*ujamaa*) on the fourth, purpose (*nia*) on the fifth, creativity (*kuumba*) the sixth, and faith (*imani*) on the last day.

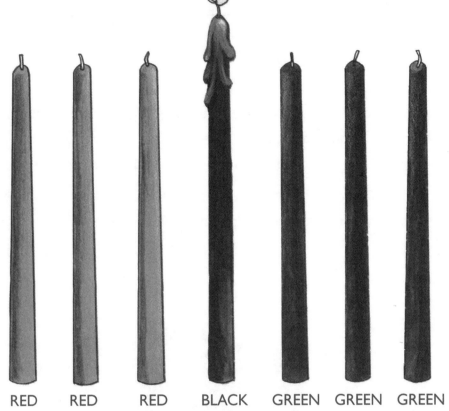

RED   RED   RED   BLACK   GREEN   GREEN   GREEN

THE *MISHUMAA SABA* OR SEVEN CANDLES (ONE BLACK, THREE RED, AND THREE GREEN) SYMBOLIZE THE *NGUZO SABA*, OR THE SEVEN PRINCIPLES THAT ARE CELEBRATED DURING KWANZAA.

Kwanzaa Connections

Set up your kinara with these other symbols of the African American community:

* the *mkeka,* the straw mat on which everything sits, symbolizes tradition and history, the foundation on which the community is built

* the *muhindi,* dried ears of corn that symbolize the children and the future

* the *Kikombe cha Umoja,* or the cup of unity from which everyone drinks each night

* the *bendera,* the flag showing three horizontal stripes of black (symbolizing the African people), red (the struggle for equality and human rights), and green (symbolizing the fertility and prosperity that grows from Kwaanza values)

To learn more about the meaning of the holiday read *Kwanzaa: Everything You Always Wanted to Know But Didn't Know Where to Ask,* by Cedric McClester.

NATURAL CANDLEHOLDER

Make a candleholder that celebrates nature and the changing seasons! Cut a small circular or oval base from heavy cardboard or wood (ask an adult to cut a round slice of a large branch). Glue on a candle and whatever beautiful nature finds — pinecones, acorns, colorful rocks, dried flowers — you've collected. Use it as a centerpiece for your dinner table.

✳ Sound Effects! ✳

When's the last time you were told to make a lot of noise? Maybe never! Now's your chance. It's fun to find and make sounds. You start to think about what things actually sound like — you even hear them differently. Stalk some interesting sounds, and who knows? You may have so much fun that you'll decide to be a foley artist, enhancing the sounds in movies, or creating the sounds in computer games!

What You Need

* Cassette tapes
* Tape recorder
* Sound-makers: Use anything you have on hand!

Ahhh

Wop, bop-a-loo-bop, ba lop bam boom

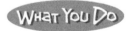

What You Do

Seek out sound and listen in new ways! Then collect the sounds on tape.

✳ Found Sounds

Travel around your house, yard, and neighborhood recording what you hear: airplanes flying overhead, birds chirping/cawing, brooms swishing, car doors slamming, car traffic, cats fighting, cats purring, crowd noises, dogs barking, doors creaking, appliances running, power tools going, rain (dripping, pounding, splashing, tapping), squirrels playing, wind in trees. What sounds did you find?

✳ Made Sounds

Experiment! Here are a few fun ideas to get you started. Once you get the hang of it, you won't need any introduction!

1. Bang on boxes, cans, drums, pots, and walls. Hammer things.

2. Cook oatmeal and record "mud pot" sounds.

3. Clang light poles, wave sheet metal to get "thunder."

4. Crinkle plastic, rustle paper, pull tape off of surfaces (a very interesting sound!)

5. Play an instrument, record the cat walking on the piano!

6. Pour seeds into a metal pot, stretch a Slinky and shake it, use coconut shells to make horse hooves sound. What else can you come up with?

clang, crinkle, rustle, pop

✳ Body Sounds

Here's a category that needs no explanation! You have a lot of sounds you already make for fun. See how many you can discover and record.

✳ **Body:** Clap your hands, play a tune on your cheek by lightly slapping your cheek with your hand; change your mouth shape to get different notes, snap your fingers, stamp your feet, tap your body, make horse galloping sounds (clap hands together, then slap right hand on thigh, then slap left hand on thigh in a slow, quick, quick rhythm)

✳ **Bodily:** burp, cough, crunch crackers, hiccup, slurp food, record your stomach growling, swallow — and on and on!

✳ **Voice:** growl, grunt, hiss, hum, scream, sigh, sing, talk, whisper, whistle. Thump your cheek for a water drip, press your lips for a fly buzz, make a very expressive raspberry!

ork, ork, ork, ork!

✳ Use your sounds!

✳ Make sound effects in a movie you create (page 26)

✳ Tell a story such as the Lion Hunt with sounds of mud, tall grass, running, etc. Or tell a story you wrote yourself, using sound effects.

✳ Make a tape for a haunted house.

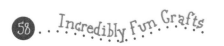

INCREDIBLE CRAFTS FROM NEAR & FAR

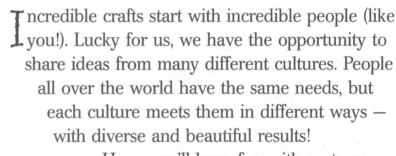

I ncredible crafts start with incredible people (like you!). Lucky for us, we have the opportunity to share ideas from many different cultures. People all over the world have the same needs, but each culture meets them in different ways — with diverse and beautiful results!

Here, you'll have fun with customs and creations from near and far, adding your original ideas to these age-old traditions. Celebrate Pysanky, the Ukrainian custom of egg decorating, make and wear American Indian clothing like Tlingit moccasins, revel in Mexican festivities by creating metal ornaments, make and play with a yo-yo unlike any you've seen before … and more! What a fabulous thing it is to enjoy our traditions and have the freedom to learn from and enjoy other people's traditions, too!

✳ Create in the Pysanky Tradition ✳

You'll be amazed at the colorful patterns you can create using wax and dyes — with an egg for your 3-D "canvas"! Pysanky (peh-SAN-key), the Ukrainian custom of egg decorating, is traditionally done in the spring, around Easter, but you can make these designs any time of year. What about giving a Pysanky-styled egg for best wishes on New Year's Day? Or, on a religious holiday about new beginnings and good wishes, or maybe on the first day of spring? Make and give one when a new baby is born, or as a special wedding gift. You can even design an egg to celebrate the first day of the school year! Whatever the occasion, experiment with simple or fancy designs as you create whatever is in your mind's eye.

What You Need

* Powdered dyes (preferable) or Easter egg dyes
* Boiling water
* Sturdy cups, glasses, or small canning jars
* White vinegar (optional)
* White-shelled eggs (fresh, not boiled. They're for decorating, not for eating!)
* Pencil
* Short candle and safety matches*
* Kistka tool or small finish nail (MAKE A KISTKA, page 63)
* Spoon
* Egg cartons
* Soft cloths

Use only with adult supervision

Eggs of Glad Tidings

This custom of decorating eggs originated in the Ukraine, a country bordered by Russia, Romania, Belarus, Moldova, Poland, and the Black Sea. There, the tradition of egg dyeing extends back thousands of years, when the carefully decorated eggs were thought to ward off evil spirits and ensure a healthy family.

Nowadays, decorated eggs are still exchanged among friends and relatives, with the designs carefully tailored to express good wishes for the recipient. A young couple planning to start a family might be given eggs decorated with chicks, hens, and roosters, while a farmer may be given an egg with wheat shafts and farming tool shapes for good luck in the harvest.

What will you wish for someone who is lucky enough to receive a Pysanky-styled egg from you?

WHAT YOU DO

WAXING THE EGG

1. Prepare the powdered dyes (EGG DYEING TIPS, page 62) by mixing each with boiling water in a jar. Let cool. Clean off the eggs and let them come to room temperature (otherwise, the eggs will "sweat" and the wax won't stick). Sketch your design on the egg in pencil. That way, you'll be sure the design you want fits, and you won't have to worry about creating the design as you wax the egg.

Egg-Dyeing Tips

✦ Spread old newspapers everywhere you'll be working, and wear an old shirt. Dyes can color more than just eggs!

✦ Check eggs for tiny cracks and bumps by holding them up to the light. Cracked eggs are more likely to break during the egg-dyeing process, and bumps are difficult to draw over.

✦ Clean eggs with a solution of white vinegar (half a cup/125 ml of water to 1 teaspoon/ 2 ml vinegar) to remove dirt and oils that won't "take" the color.

✦ Use strong, bright dyes from an art supply store or from Pysanky kits. These powdered dyes will last for many years if they're kept sealed and cool. (Regular egg dyes are not nearly as bright.) However, because these dyes are poisonous, they must be handled with care (page 65), and the dyed eggs should never be eaten. When dyeing, start with the lightest color and end with the darkest color. Add a teaspoon (5 ml) of white vinegar to the dye if it doesn't color dark enough.

Traditional Designs

Start with a basic design, dividing the egg into evenly spaced sections. One traditional design is to make endless lines of curlicues, waves, and zigzags that go around the egg and meet. Or, you might try using geometric designs like triangles, which represent air, fire, and water. Flower, tree, wheat, vine, grape, chicken, butterfly, spider, horse, and deer designs symbolize good health, love, and wealth.

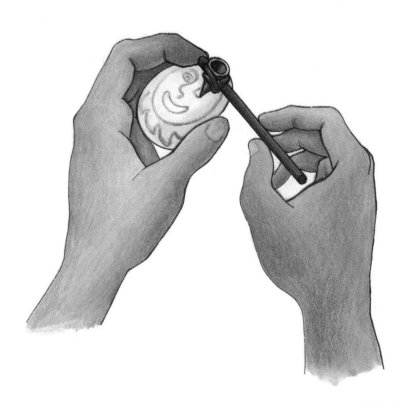

2. Light the candle (keep long sleeves and hair away from the flame!) and warm the nail head (MAKE A KISTKA, below) in the flame.

3. Dip the nail head into the pool of melted wax and quickly draw a thin line of wax on the egg wherever you want it to remain white.

4. Re-warm the nail head in the flame, dip in the melted wax again, and draw on the egg with more wax until you complete your design. Be sure to wax all the places you want to remain white on the finished egg. Let the wax dry.

DYEING THE EGG

The traditional order for using dyes is yellow, orange, red, blue, and black. But don't let that keep you from experimenting with your own color combinations! Just *start with the lightest color* and *end with the darkest.*

1. To dye the first color, use a spoon to carefully lower the egg into yellow (or other light color) dye. Let the egg soak for 5 minutes.

Make a Kistka

You can buy a kistka from a craft store, or make this homemade version using a pencil and a very small finishing nail. Push the nail through the eraser of the pencil as shown. To use, warm the nail head, dip into wax, and draw on the egg.

The traditional kistka tool has a funnel about an inch long that's attached to a 5" (12.5 cm) stick. You warm the reservoir of wax in the funnel and draw on the egg with the pointed tip.

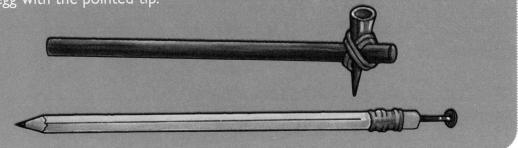

2. Remove the egg with the spoon and let it dry about 5 minutes (you may need to dab it with tissues). When dry, apply wax over all the areas you want to remain yellow.

3. Now dye the egg in orange (or the next chosen color). After the egg dries, apply wax to all the areas you want to stay orange. Use the same method to dye the egg in red, blue, and black (or other colors of your choice), always covering the newly dyed color in wax. Let the egg dry completely.

4. To remove the wax, hold the egg for a couple of seconds in front of the candle flame until the wax on that one part is melted. (Or, if you don't want to use a flame, try an electric hair dryer, *away* from the sink, of course!) Dab off the melted wax quickly and gently with a soft cloth.

5. Continue melting the wax on other parts of the egg until it's completely removed. You now have a beautiful egg to give as a gift or to use as a decoration!

PRESERVING THE EGG

Traditional Pysanky eggs still have the raw egg inside, but because the egg could go bad (and cause an awful smell — *pee-yew!*), it's a good idea to blow out the egg. You have to do this *after* dyeing, or else the empty egg will float in the dye. Practice on a couple of plain, undyed raw eggs first, until you get the knack of blowing out the egg using a straw. *Poison Alert!* Don't use the egg for food, because the poisonous dye may have seeped inside.

1. Carefully prick a hole in each end of the egg with an opened paper clip, needle, or pin. Make one hole a little larger than the other.

2. Cut a drinking straw into about three pieces. Use one short straw piece to blow air into the smaller hole in the egg. *Note: It's important to use a straw so your mouth doesn't touch the poisonous dye.* The gooey egg will ooze out the larger hole and into the bowl.

3. Blow until the inside is empty. Let the egg dry inside and out.

Adding Pizzazz

Egg-ceptional Idea

Make a nest for your finished eggs out of feathers, twigs, and vines, with a few scraps of yarn or dryer lint for color and texture.

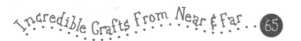

✳ Make Mexican Aluminum Ornaments ✳

These beautiful ornaments from Mexico are traditionally made from tin. You can buy lightweight tin from craft stores or make yours out of recycled aluminum (from disposable pie pans, bread and cake tins, or roasting pans). Use your ornaments however you like — to decorate windows, the walls in a bedroom or kitchen, or to hang on a holiday tree.

What You Need

* Scrap paper and pencil
* Scissors
* Aluminum, recycled from disposable pans, or store-bought tin sheets
* Cardboard
* Nail
* Wire or paper clips

What You Do

1. Draw a favorite shape of an animal, sun or moon, flower, or other object on scrap paper. Once you have a design you like, cut it out and trace the shape onto the aluminum.

2. Cut out the aluminum design. Place the cutout on a scrap of cardboard for padding. Using the nail, make impressions in the soft metal.

3. With the nail, poke a small hole at the top of the ornament. Insert wire or a paper clip for hanging.

Punched-Metal Frame

Bend aluminum around a homemade cardboard picture frame. Use a nail to punch a design or write a person's name, then tape a favorite photo to the frame back. Give it to someone special.

Making Do!

In Mexico, many beautiful crafts are made from tin, in part because tin is inexpensive and easy to work with. Originally, the indigenous people (the native Mexicans) used silver and gold to make their metal objects, but when the Spanish invaded Mexico in 1519 and took much of the valuable gold, the craftspeople and metalworkers improvised by using tin. Since that time, Mexicans have continued using tin, making beautiful trays, pitchers, mirrors, and candelabras wonderfully decorated with birds, animals, flowers, and other shapes.

How can you adapt what you have on hand? Here's one idea: The aluminum tops from frozen juice containers have rounded edges that are ideal for ornaments. Use a nail to poke a design of holes in the lids for light to shine through! It's amazing what you can do when you use your imagination and work with what you have.

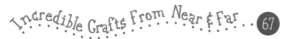

✳ American Indian Dream Catchers ✳

Have you ever seen light dancing on the dewdrops on a spider web in the early morning? Dream catchers are a tradition from many different Indian tribes, each with its own legend and interpretation. The Ojibwa trace this custom back to the very beginning of their history when Spider Woman (or Grandmother Spider) spun magical webs on the tops of cradle boards to ensure babies a peaceful slumber. The web caught the bad dreams, but let good dreams slide right through the center hole. Eventually, as the people dispersed, she taught the sisters, moms, and grandmothers how to make them using willow hoops and sinew or plants.

Among some other American Indian tribes, dream catchers are thought to hold the destiny of the future, capturing the good visions in the web of life and allowing the bad to escape through. Now, you can make them, too. As with all cultural artifacts, dream catchers are to be treated with respect.

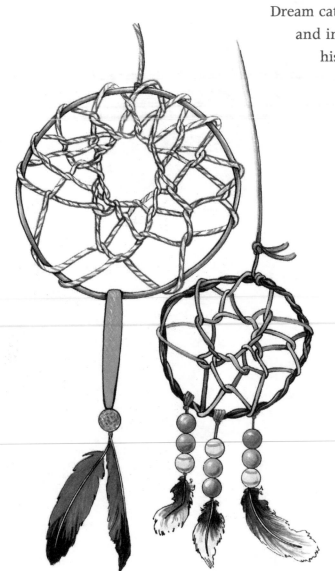

What You Need

* Rings, about 4" to 10" (10 to 25 cm) in diameter, one per dream catcher. Try *metal rings,* from cardboard-sided cocoa containers, *sealing rings* from yogurt or cottage cheese containers (glue the split ends together), *plastic lids,* cut into a ring, *vines,* shaped into a ring (page 100), *basket reeds* or *craft hoops.* If you wish, wind some colorful yarn around the ring to decorate.
* Yarn or string, about 3 yards (3 m)
* Beads, feathers, and small shells with holes (optional)

1. Tie one end of the yarn or string to the ring and wind it loosely back and forth across it eight to 12 times until you're back to the beginning.

2. When you get back to the first loop, pull the yarn through that loop, but not around the outer ring. Continue around the circle, pulling the yarn through each of the loops in turn to make a web.

3. Continue around the ring again, going through the new loops you just created. Pull the yarn tight until there's only a small circular space left in the center. (You may need to go around more times if your ring is large.)

4. Tie the end of the yarn securely, leaving a long end for hanging.

Wondrous Web Decorations

Add personal touches to your dream catcher. Try these, or your own clever decorating ideas!

✳ String small beads on the yarn as you form the web pattern.

✳ Tie yarn on the bottom of the ring and string beads on it, knotting the yarn at the bottom.

✳ Slide beads on feathers and glue the quills to the end of the yarn tied to the bottom of the ring.

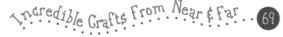

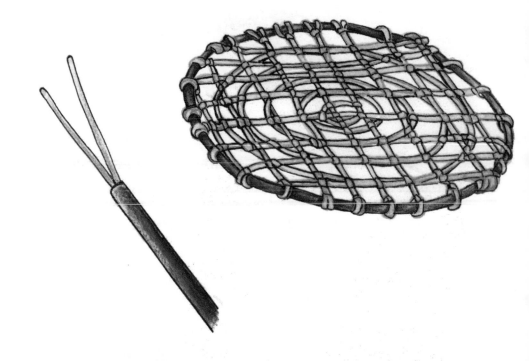

Dream Catcher Earrings

Make miniature dream catchers to wear as earrings or to hang as small ornaments. You'll need a little plastic curtain ring or the cutoff circular end of a plastic bubble-blower wand, a blunt sewing needle, and 18" (45 cm) of dental floss. (If you use flavored dental floss, you'll have good-smelling earrings!) Loop around the outside nine times and use the needle to help you feed the floss through the very tiny places. Decorate with tiny beads.

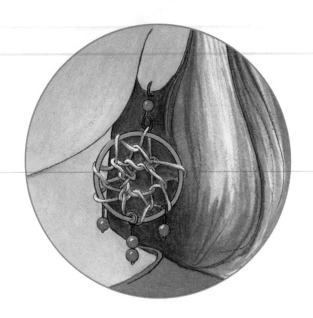

Play Hoop and Pole

This American Indian game is great fun to play, but takes good coordination to do well. Large hoops were traditionally made from bent branches and rawhide was woven across in a crisscross pattern, similar to the way a dream catcher is made. The poles were bendable branches about 3' (1 m) long. To play, one team tosses the hoops in the air and the other team tries to catch them on the ends of their poles, spearing as close as possible to the center. If a hoop is caught, the pole team keeps it. If a hoop is missed, two hoops are returned to the hoop team. The team that gains all of the hoops first is the winner.

✳ Make an Iñupaq Yo-Yo ✳

When you hear the word *yo-yo*, you probably think of the wheel on string you roll up and down from your finger. You're right! But there's more to it. Though the word *yo-yo* was coined in the 1920s in America, the toy has been around for much longer. Kids played with yo-yos in ancient Egypt 5,000 years ago!

This yo-yo is a toy that's similar to a useful tool traditionally used by the Inuit people of Alaska. It's fun, and furry — and is a challenge to play!

What You Do

MAKING THE YO-YO

1. Trace the yo-yo pattern (page 72) on the paper. Cut it out. Trace the pattern two times on the back of the fur or fabric; cut out both pieces.

2. Working with one piece, fold the fake fur in half (so it's inside out). Sew up one side. Sew one end of the rope to the top.

3. Turn the fur right side out. Stuff the inside with seeds or pebbles.

What You Need

* Ruler, paper, pencil, scissors, for pattern
* Two pieces of fake fur or strong cloth
* Fabric scissors
* Large sewing needles
* Thread or dental floss
* Rope (MAKE YARN ROPE!, page 74) or yarn, 1 yard (1 m)
* Unpopped popcorn, dried peas or other dry seeds, pebbles
* Empty thread spool or piece of wood or shell, with a center hole, for the handle

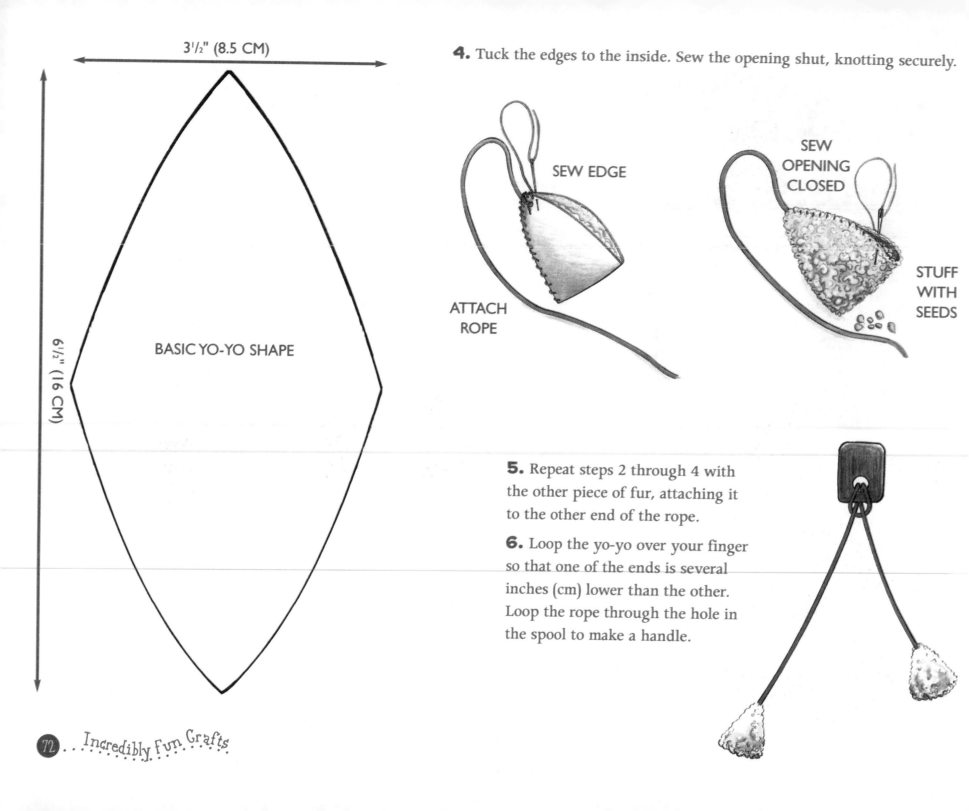

3½" (8.5 CM)

6½" (16 CM)

BASIC YO-YO SHAPE

4. Tuck the edges to the inside. Sew the opening shut, knotting securely.

SEW EDGE

ATTACH ROPE

SEW OPENING CLOSED

STUFF WITH SEEDS

5. Repeat steps 2 through 4 with the other piece of fur, attaching it to the other end of the rope.

6. Loop the yo-yo over your finger so that one of the ends is several inches (cm) lower than the other. Loop the rope through the hole in the spool to make a handle.

Incredibly Fun Crafts

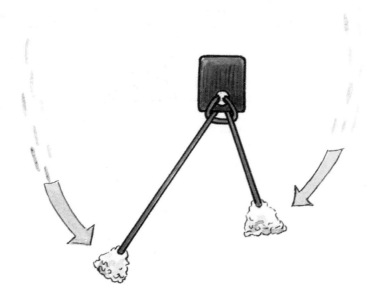

Yo! Let's Yo-Yo!

To play, get one end to go whizzing around *clockwise* and the other to go *counterclockwise* vertically in front of you. It takes a while to get good at this, but it's lots of fun when you do!

Yo-Yoing Method #1
1. Spread out the yo-yo on the ground or a bench.
2. Lift up the handle quickly and evenly as you stand up.
3. Move your hand up and down slightly to keep the yo-yo moving.

Adding Pizzazz

Yo-Yo Add-Ons

The traditional Inuit yo-yo is made of sealskin filled with moss and decorated with fringes of hide. You could sew some 1" to 2" (2.5 to 5 cm) fringes of leather or ribbons on your yo-yo and watch them wiggle in the breeze as you twirl it. Or, make the furry ends into creatures by gluing or sewing on features. Add wiggly eyes that will "look around" as the yo-yo whizzes past you!

MAKE YARN ROPE!

No string on hand? No problem! Just make your own. All you need is a friend and some odds and ends of yarn.

1. Decide how long you want your rope to be. Cut two or more pieces of yarn twice as long as that length. (Note: Using different colors of yarn makes it easier to tell if you have twisted the yarn enough, and it's also very beautiful!)

2. Tie one end of each yarn piece to a post or doorknob. Hold the other end of the yarn bundle tightly and start twisting the yarn until the rope is very tight. Always twist in the same direction, and don't let go!

3. Ask a friend to hold the twisted yarn firmly, halfway between you and the doorknob.

4. Bring the end you've been twisting around to the tied end, keeping it straight and tight.

5. Ask your helper to let go of the yarn. Watch as the yarn magically twists on itself. You just discovered what makes rope so strong! You can help it to twist properly by pulling your hands gently down the length of the twist. Tie a knot at each end of the rope.

Yo-Yoing Method #2

1. Hold the handle in your right hand.
2. With your left hand, throw the long end up so it goes clockwise in front of you. Keep it going by moving your right hand up and down slightly.
3. Get the short end going by holding it in your left hand and throwing it down at the same speed that the long one is going, but in the opposite direction. The two ends will whiz past each other as you continue to move your right hand up and down!

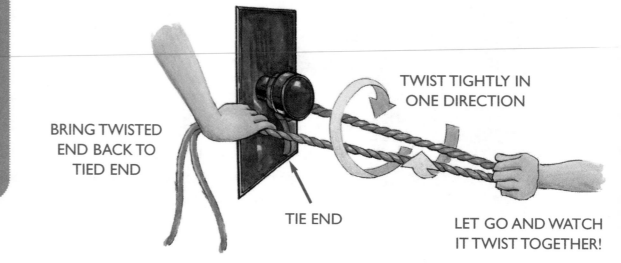

BRING TWISTED END BACK TO TIED END

TWIST TIGHTLY IN ONE DIRECTION

TIE END

LET GO AND WATCH IT TWIST TOGETHER!

 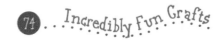

✳ Stitch (& Wear!) ✳ American Indian Moccasins

Level of Challenge: 2
⏰ 2 to 3 hours for moccasins
1 to 2 hours for beading (optional)

Make yourself comfortable footwear, made to fit you perfectly and decorated with your own cool designs!

WESTERN DAKOTA MOCCASINS

Moccasins made in one piece per foot! What could be simpler?

What You Need

* Paper grocery bag or other stiff paper, folded in half
* Ruler, pencil, craft scissors, for making pattern
* Leather, felt, or vinyl fabric, two 12" x 15" (30 x 37.5 cm) scraps (one per moccasin)
* Fabric scissors*
* Awl or hammer and nail (SEW EASY, page 77)*
* Yarn, leather cord, or rawhide
* Leatherwork needle or other strong sewing needle with a large eye
* Clothespin
* Beads and glue (optional)

*Use only with adult supervision

What You Do

MAKING THE PATTERN AND CUTTING THE FABRIC

1. Place one foot on the folded paper so the instep (inner side) is about ¹/₂" (1 cm) in from the fold. Holding the pencil vertically, trace around your foot. (See next page.)

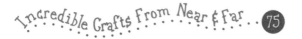

2. Because your foot is 3-D, you need to make the pattern longer and wider than your footprint for the moccasin to fit. From the fold, draw a line ³/₄" (2 cm) larger than your footprint on all sides. Make the heel square.

3. Cut the paper pattern (don't cut the fold). Open the pattern (you'll have the same shape on either side of the fold). Place it on the leather or vinyl and trace around it, then cut it out. Using the same pattern, cut out a moccasin for the other foot.

SEWING THE MOCCASIN

1. Fold the leather so the good side is out. Poke holes and stitch around the toe and down the outside, but not across the bottom. Be sure the fold is to the inside of your foot for each moccasin.

2. Cut a slit in the topside of the moccasin to make the opening for your foot.

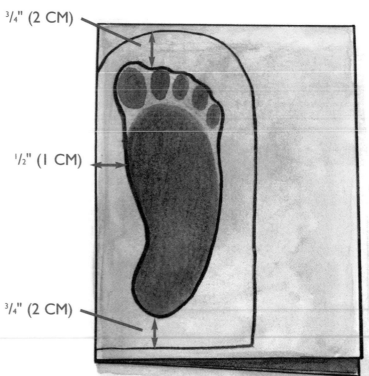

³/₄" (2 CM)

¹/₂" (1 CM)

³/₄" (2 CM)

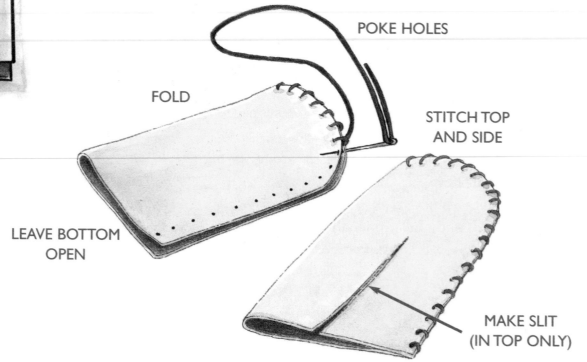

POKE HOLES

FOLD

STITCH TOP AND SIDE

LEAVE BOTTOM OPEN

MAKE SLIT (IN TOP ONLY)

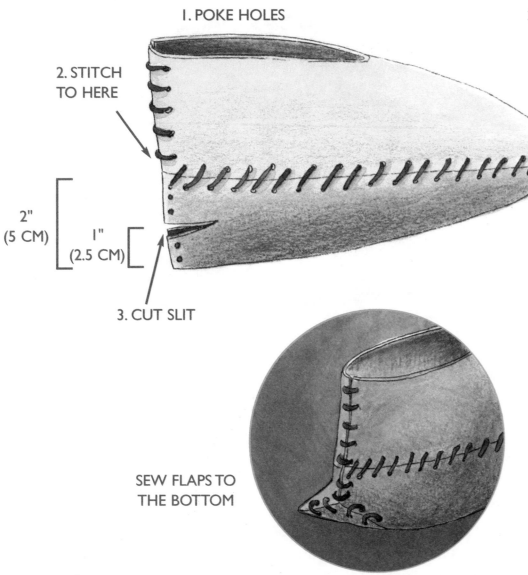

1. POKE HOLES

2. STITCH TO HERE

2" (5 CM)

1" (2.5 CM)

3. CUT SLIT

SEW FLAPS TO THE BOTTOM

3. Try on the moccasin. Pinch the heel closed with the clothespin. Take off the moccasin and mark with pencil where the seam (joining) should be. Cut off any excess leather and punch holes through both back pieces. Stitch the heel seam from the top down to 2" (5 cm) from the bottom.

4. About 1" (2.5 cm) from the bottom, cut a 1" (2.5 cm) slit on both sides of the sole. Fold down the heel and sew the two flaps you just made to the bottom of the moccasin, punching any additional holes as necessary

5. Try on your moccasin. Enlarge the top opening if needed. Fold down the top edge of the opening and sew or glue on decorative beads, if you like (see BEADING BASICS, page 80).

Crafter's Clues

Sew Easy

To make it easy to sew through the thick leather or vinyl, poke holes about ¹/₂" (1 cm) for the stitches through both leather pieces as shown with an *awl* (a sharp pointed tool) or with a hammer and nail. As with all sharp tools, use only with adult supervision, please.

Adding Pizzazz

Double-Soled Moccasins

Trace around the finished moccasin onto another piece of leather and cut just inside the line. Slip the insole into the moccasin. Repeat for the other moccasin.

TLINGIT-STYLE MOCCASINS

Make yourself a pair of fancy moccasins just like those worn by the Tlingit people, who live in southeastern Alaska.

What You Need

Same supplies as for the WESTERN DAKOTA MOCCASINS (page 75), plus:
* Felt pieces, for the vamp
* Safety pins

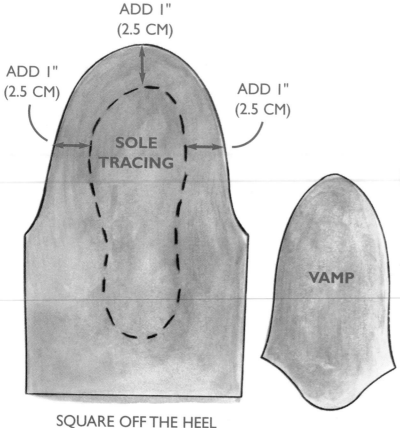

ADD 1" (2.5 CM)

ADD 1" (2.5 CM)

ADD 1" (2.5 CM)

SOLE TRACING

VAMP

SQUARE OFF THE HEEL

What You Do

MAKING THE PATTERN AND CUTTING THE FABRIC

1. Trace your foot onto the paper bag and draw the moccasin bottom pattern shown. The pattern needs to be about 1" (2.5 cm) longer than each of your feet and about 1" (2.5 cm) wider on the top and side of the toes. Make the heel square.

2. Cut out the pattern, and label it. Trace it onto the vinyl or leather, and cut it out. Flip the pattern over to use for the other foot, and cut out the leather.

3. Draw the *vamp* (the moccasin top) pattern, sizing it to fit over the toe portion of the sole as shown. Then trace it onto the felt and cut it out.

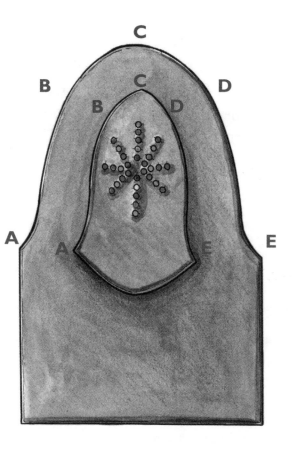

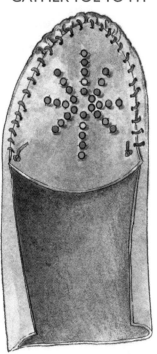

GATHER TOE TO FIT

SEWING THE MOCCASIN

1. Hold the vamp in place on the moccasin bottom as shown. Using safety pins, pin the A, B, C, D, and E points on the vamp to the corresponding points on the moccasin bottom.

2. For easy sewing (page 77), poke holes about $^1/_2$" (1 cm) apart through both pieces from A to E, using an awl or hammer and nail. Stitch between A and E, "gathering" the toe material together to fit and making small tucks in the bottom piece. Knot the end.

3. Try on the moccasin. Pinch the heel closed with the clothespin. Take off the moccasin and mark with a pencil where the seam should be. Cut off any excess leather down to 1" (2.5 cm) from the bottom and punch holes through both sides for the seam. Stitch the heel seam from the top down to 1" (2.5 cm) from the bottom. Cut a slit as shown on both sides, below the stitching.

4. Fold the heel down and sew the two flaps you just made to the bottom. Cut the excess leather that hangs down into a fringe that will erase your tracks as you walk!

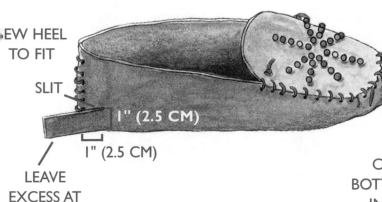

SEW HEEL TO FIT

SLIT

1" (2.5 CM)

1" (2.5 CM)

LEAVE EXCESS AT BOTTOM

SEW FLAPS TO BOTTOM

CUT EXCESS BOTTOM LEATHER INTO FRINGE

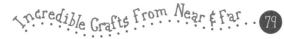

Incredible Crafts From Near & Far . . **79**

◄ Crafter's Clues ►

Vamp Decor

You can use leather or vinyl for the vamp, but felt is much easier to decorate with tiny beads. Do any beadwork *before* sewing the moccasin together. See BEADING BASICS, right.

Ways of Life

The Tlingit people live along the water, on the many islands and inland passages of southeastern Alaska, and are known for their beautiful woodcarvings seen on masks and totem poles, intricate baskets and clothing, and wonderful dances and songs. Artistic expression is very important to them. In what ways do you like to express yourself best?

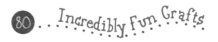

Adding Pizzazz

Beading Basics

Put beads on your felt top (vamp) for the Tlingit moccasins, or on pieces of felt that you cut out and glue onto your Western Dakota moccasins (page 75). Use a very thin needle that can pass through the tiny beads of your choice.

1. Plan your design and draw it lightly in pencil (use chalk for dark felt).

2. Thread the needle and double-knot the end. Sew through the felt from the back, so the needle comes out where you want to start your design.

3. Slip three to five beads on the needle and slide them down the thread to the felt. Place them along the design and put the needle through the felt exactly where they end. Bring the needle up through the felt again to add more beads. Continue until your design is complete.

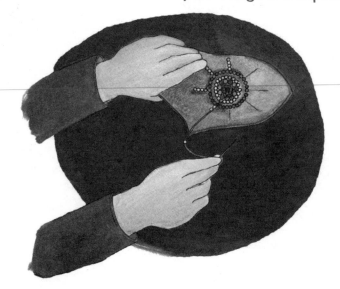

Fur-Lined Moccasins

1. Use fake fur from an old coat or slippers, or buy a remnant at a fabric store.

2. Decide where you want to place the fake fur. Cut fur strips 1/2" (1 cm) wide and long enough to cover these areas (you can overlap pieces if necessary). Sew or glue in place.

3. Put your moccasins on your feet and dance around!

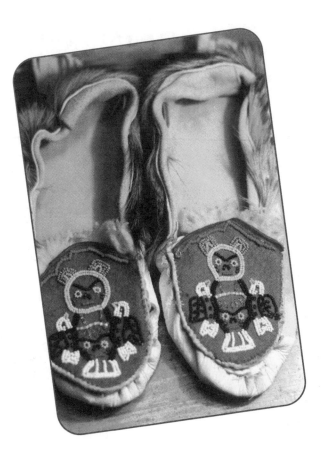

Quills & Beads

American Indians are respected for their beautiful beadwork. Initially, the Indians created beautiful designs on moccasins with porcupine quills. Then bright beads, received through trading with westerners, replaced the quills. Present-day Tlingit people make intricate eagles, frogs, and other animal designs with beads.

Seams Good to Me

Notice anything about the seams on these moccasins? Well, on each one, the seam between the sole and the top of the shoe doesn't touch the ground when you walk. That way, the seam threads don't get worn out by rubbing on the ground. Can you think of any other advantages? Do you think it makes them more comfortable?

Some American Indian footwear has thin strips of leather sewn in between the two layers of each seam to make them waterproof. As the stitches are pulled tight, the thin strip gets squished and it fills in all the spaces, eliminating the little cracks where water might seep in. This traditional method requires sewing through three thicknesses — so you might want to keep it simple and just stay out of the rain!

✳ Magical Peek-In Sugar Eggs ✳

There's magic in creating a delicate egg out of crumbly sugar, and there's more magic when the scene is finished and you can peek into the miniature world you've created! Sugar eggs are a traditional northern European craft. They're fun to make year-round, not just in springtime, and they'll last for years if stored in a cool, dry place.

Shaping the sugar & cutting the peephole

What You Need

* Plastic egg, 3" to 7" (7.5 to 17.5 cm)
* 2 egg whites (use powdered egg whites mixed with warm water if you plan to taste your egg)
* 5 lb (2.2 kg) granulated sugar
* Large mixing bowl
* Clean cloths
* Butter knife
* Cardboard scraps
* Cookie sheet
* Sharp knife*
* Spoon

*Use only with adult supervision

What You Do

This recipe makes five big eggs or 15 small eggs. The shells are very delicate, so take your time and handle them gently. If you plan on eating (even tasting!) your eggs, use only powdered egg whites — not fresh eggs, which must be cooked before being eaten (that includes nibbles!). Wash your hands, utensils, and all surfaces with soap and hot water when handling eggs.

1. Clean and dry both sections of the egg mold.

2. Mix the egg whites with the sugar in a large bowl by hand until the mix feels like wet sand. Use immediately, before the mixture dries and hardens. Cover the remaining mix with a wet cloth to keep it damp.

3. Pack the molds tightly to the top with the sugar mix. Level off any excess sugar using the straight side of a butter knife.

4. Place a cardboard piece on the flat side of the sugar-filled mold. Turn the egg half over quickly; place on the cookie sheet.

5. Remove the plastic mold very carefully and inspect the egg half to make sure it's smooth and uncracked. (If it's damaged, return the sugar mixture to the bowl and try again.) Make as many top and bottom sets as you like.

6. Cut through the last inch (2.5 cm) or so of the more pointed end of each egg half with the knife. Leave the cutoff end in place. This will eventually be the peep-hole you'll look into when the egg is done.

7. Let the sugar harden for 1½ hours, or ask permission to bake it in an oven at 200°F (95°C) for six to 12 minutes. When done, the outside should be crusty, and the inside soft enough to be scooped out.

8. Remove the peephole section. Hold the hardened egg half in one hand and use a spoon to scoop out the center, leaving a shell about ½" (1 cm) thick. Don't make the shell too thin or it may crack. Scoop out all the remaining halves.

9. Let the hollow egg halves harden overnight.

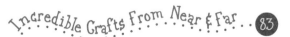

Decorating & creating the scene

* Pastry bags and decorating tips, one for each color, or zip-locking plastic bags with a small hole cut in one corner
* Icing, several light colors (COLORFUL ICING, page 85)
* Rubber bands
* Small candies shaped like birds, bunnies, eggs, flowers, or trees
* Chocolate chips, jelly beans, jelly fruits, Red-Hots, sprinkles, or other small, colorful candies
* Granulated sugar, dyed with food coloring
* Colorful ribbons

Crafter's Clues

Decorating Tips

◆ Remember to face the scene toward the opening.

◆ Don't overdecorate the "sky," as candies may fall off when the egg half is turned upside-down. Let the icing harden completely before turning the egg over.

WHAT YOU DO

1. Fill each pastry bag or sandwich bag with a different color of icing. Secure the ends with rubber bands.

2. Squeeze a little icing inside the bottom half of the egg. It will work as "glue" to anchor the candies where you want them. (If you're using a sandwich bag, you can shape the icing with a fork or butter knife.)

3. Create a scene with the candies and icing. Decorate the inside top of the egg as a ceiling or sky.

4. Squeeze icing around the rim of the shell's bottom half. Gently place the top half on it.

5. Cover the outside seam with icing and candies. Decorate the outside of the egg.

6. Peek in! Does the little world you created seem magically larger?

Colorful icing

Prepare this icing in advance and store tightly covered in the refrigerator. This recipe makes enough icing for two sugar eggs and fills one pastry bag. Experiment with far-out colors!

WHAT YOU NEED

* egg white (use powdered egg white mixed with warm water if you plan to taste it)
* 1¹⁄₃ cup (325 ml) confectioners' sugar
* Cream of tartar
* Mixing bowl
* Electric mixer
* Food coloring, different colors

Little Worlds

Here are a few ideas for egg scenes to inspire you:

* A beach scene with a blue-green icing ocean and brown sugar sand scattered with candy seashells. Make a big sun on the egg's roof.

* A pond surrounded by candy flowers, with a path through woods.

* An egg scene of Antarctica! Use blue sugar on the roof to make a glacier cave or underwater scene, and white frosting for snow.

* Small half eggshells can be made into boats or nests.

   (For more on making miniature worlds, see page 24.)

WHAT YOU DO

1. Combine the egg white, confectioners' sugar, and a pinch of cream of tartar in a mixing bowl.

2. Beat the mixture until the icing is fluffy and smooth, about 7 minutes.

3. Mix a few drops of food coloring into each batch of icing.

Day of the Dead

Europeans aren't the only crafters who use sugar in sculpture. The people of Mexico make intricate sugar skulls every November 1 and 2 for Dia de Los Muertos, or "Day of the Dead," a centuries-old celebration in which friends or relatives who have died are honored in a joyous memorial. Beautiful displays of flowers, fruit, vegetables, bread, candles, and other items are set out with the sugar skulls in altars that celebrate life and remember loved ones.

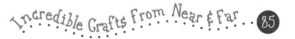

INCREDIBLE KNOTS, WEAVES & NOT KNOTS

History is a long rope, and you're the next knot in it! When you do these projects, you're using skills that have been handed down from generation to generation — for thousands of years! Make friendship bracelets like people do in Mexico, Guatemala, and Japan. Weave headbands and belts on a simple loom you make yourself, learn to braid leather, and knit yarn on your fingers. As you explore the ways of crafters long ago, you'll create your own cool stuff for today!

✳ Make Friendship Bracelets ✳

The knots in these bracelets symbolize the bond of friendship. Kids the world over make them — and so can you!

In Japan, friendship bracelets are called "wish bracelets," because you make a wish when you put the bracelet on. When the bracelet wears out and falls off, your wish comes true!

BASIC SIX-STRAND BRACELET

What You Need

* Embroidery thread or acrylic yarn, various colors
* Scissors
* Pushpin

Crafter's Clues

Bracelet-Making Tips

◆ Master the basic bracelet (right) before trying the trickier V's and diamonds. For an even easier knotted bracelet, start with just three strands.

◆ Keep the threads from getting tangled at the bottom by stopping from time to time and sorting them out.

◆ Make each knot the same tightness to give a uniform pattern.

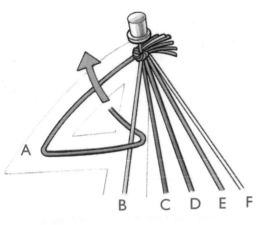

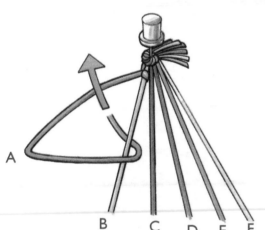

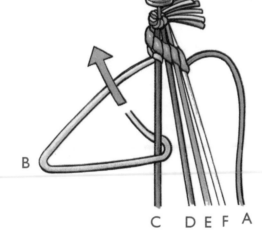

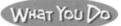
1. Cut six strings of embroidery thread about 18" (45 cm) long, or four times the length you want the bracelet to be.

2. Decide on the order of colors for your bracelet. Then, knot the strings together at one end and attach to a sturdy surface. Smooth the strings out, so they don't overlap.

3. The string on the far left is the *working string* — the sting you tie with. In this case, A. Take it in one hand and hold the next string (B) firmly in the other. Make a knot shaped like a "4" with string A by going *across* B, then go back *under* B and up. Pull the working string to the top to make a tight knot. The knot will be the color of the working string, and will cover the underneath string.

4. Repeat step 3 with the same working string (A) and the same underneath string (B), so that you make a second forward knot on the same string, below the first knot.

5. Repeat steps 3 and 4 with the same working string, but this time with the third string (C) as the underneath string. Then continue across, using the same working string (A), knotting it twice over each of the other strings, until you have a diagonal stripe.

6. Make a second stripe, using string B — now on the far left — as the new working string. For the third row, string C will be the working string, and so on.

7. Continue until you run out of string. Tie it on your own or a friend's wrist — and don't forget to make a wish!

Crafter's Clues

Knot So Secure

I like to use a pushpin to attach my starting knot to an old tabletop, but you can also tape the yarn to a board, safety-pin it to your shoelace, or slip the knot under the clip on a clipboard that you can carry with you anywhere.

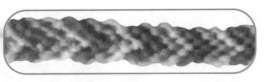

V-DESIGN BRACELET

Begin this bracelet the same way you did the BASIC SIX-STRAND BRACELET (page 87), but use two strands each of three colors. You can use any colors you choose. To make it easier to learn the pattern, try the colors shown for your first bracelet.

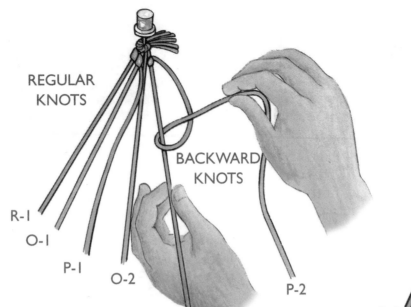

REGULAR KNOTS

BACKWARD KNOTS

R-1
O-1
P-1
O-2
R-2
P-2

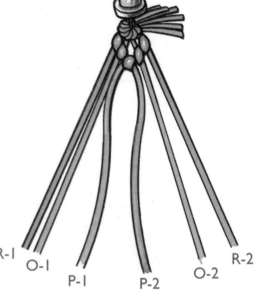

R-1
O-1
P-1
P-2
O-2
R-2

PURPLE-1
(P-1)

RED-1
(R-1)

ORANGE-1
(O-1)

ORANGE-2
(O-2)

RED-2
(R-2)

PURPLE-2
(P-2)

What You Do

1. Starting with the far left string (sound familiar?), knot P-1 over R-1 twice; then, knot P-1 over O-1 twice.

2. Now, working with the string on the far *right,* knot P-2 over R-2 twice with a *backward knot* (the regular knot in reverse). Then, knot P-2 over O-2 with a backward knot twice.

3. Knot P-2 over P-1 with a backward knot twice, to connect at the center. You have made your first V!

4. Repeat with R-1 and R-2, the new working strings, followed by O-1 and O-2. Then continue the pattern, starting again with P-1 and P-2, until you run out of string.

Knot Know-How

When you are making a diagonal row from left to right, you always use a regular knot. When you make a diagonal row from right to left, you always use a backward knot. Be sure to pull the knots tight each time so the pattern shows up better.

X'S AND DIAMONDS

What You Do

1. Begin the same way as for the V-DESIGN BRACELET (page 89). Make a purple V row as shown.

2. To fill in each triangle on the sides of the X, knot R-2 over O-2 twice with a backward knot; then, knot R-1 over O-1 twice with a regular knot.

3. To make the bottom of the X, knot P-2 over O-2 twice with a regular knot. Then, knot P-2 over R-2 twice with a regular knot. Knot P-1 over O-1 twice with a backward knot; then knot P-1 over R-1 twice with a backward knot. You have made one X!

4. To make the center of the diamond, knot O-1 over O-2 twice with a regular knot. Then knot O-2 over R-2 twice with a regular knot. Knot O-1 over R-1 twice with a backward knot. Then, knot R-1 over R-2 twice with a regular knot.

5. Start at step 1 again, making another V row, and you have one diamond. Keep going as long as you want!

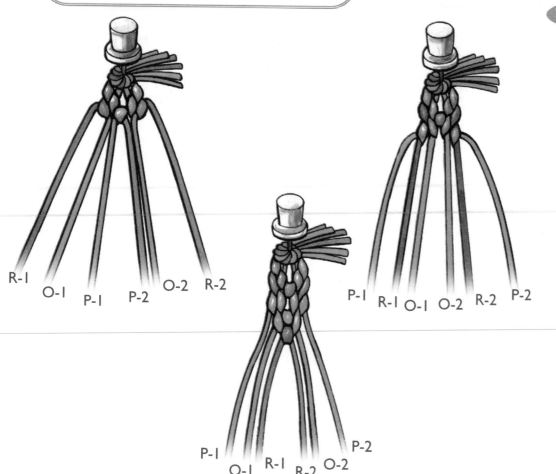

R-1   O-1   P-1   P-2   O-2   R-2

P-1   O-1   R-1   R-2   O-2   P-2

P-1   R-1   O-1   O-2   R-2   P-2

Trick-Braided Leather ✳

Make yourself a belt, a bracelet, or a choker using this surprising method of braiding, without cutting through either end of the leather.

What You Need

* Leather strip, 1" (2.5 cm) wide, about a third longer than you want the final belt, necklace, or bracelet to be (so, if your wrist is 6"/15 cm around, cut an 8"/20 cm strip of leather; if your waist is 21"/52.5 cm, cut a 28"/70 cm length strip)
* Sharp scissors, for cutting thin leather
* Craft or utility knife*, for cutting thick leather
* Clothespin

Use only with adult supervision

What You Do

1. Cut two long, evenly spaced slits in the leather strip, stopping about 1" (2.5 cm) from each end. Cut two notches near the top of the strip and an oval hole near the bottom so that later you can fasten the ends together.

2. Start braiding from one end of the leather. Braid it six times tightly (left to middle, right to middle, repeating three times). See BRAIDING PRACTICE, page 92. Untangle the unbraided end.

Be a *Trenzador*

In North and South America, many intricate kinds of braids and knots were made by frontierspeople and cowboys for horse-riding equipment. You may not have a horse to make special stuff for, but you can still become a trenzador (that's Spanish for "braider"). The skill was brought from Spain in 1519 when Hernán Cortés came with horses and horse handlers to the Americas in what is now central Mexico. Cortés learned about chocolate from the Aztecs — but they drank a very different brew than the hot chocolate of today!

3. Braid six more times and untangle again for the choker; for the belt, you'll continue braiding and untangling for a bit more. Make the braiding as tight as you can, so you'll have space at the bottom to untangle after each braid. When you run out of room, loosen the tight braiding so it fills the space evenly.

4. When you're finished, put the notched end into the oval end to fasten your belt, bracelet, or necklace.

1. Tie three pieces of rope together at one end and place them on a table.

2. Take the far left piece and bring it to the middle. Then, take the far right piece and bring it to the middle.

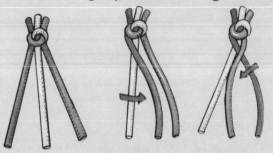

3. Repeat left to middle, right to middle.

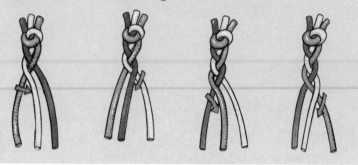

Crafter's Clues

Tangle Trick

Because the ends are not loose as in regular braiding, they can be difficult to untangle. To make untangling easier, put a clothespin firmly on the end of the braided part to make sure you don't accidentally undo the braids that you want. Then, feed the bottom end through the slits and untwist the leather until there are no more tangles.

CLOTHESPIN HERE

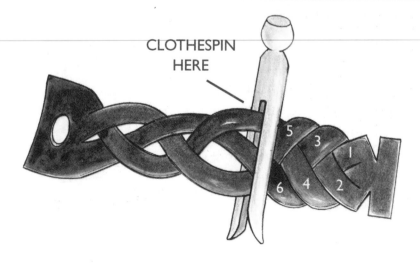

✳ Make a Homemade Loom! ✳

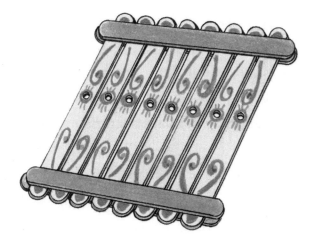

Looms are used around the world to make cloth, rugs, blankets, shawls, and wall decorations. Guatemalan women use a loom similar to the one here to weave colorful strips of cloth. Their "back-strap" looms make strips about 6" (15 cm) wide. Sewn together, they make a wide cloth for clothing.

Colonial settlers used small portable looms almost like the one you're making. A boy could weave his own shoelaces, and a girl might weave her own hair ribbons.

Use craft or Popsicle sticks to make your own small loom, then use it to create colorful belts and headband weavings!

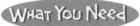
WHAT YOU NEED

* 8 to 15 craft or Popsicle sticks plus 4 more for supports
* Small cordless drill with ⅛" (2.5 mm) drill bits*
* C-clamp (optional)
* Glue or glue gun
* Colored pens or pencils
  Use only with adult supervision

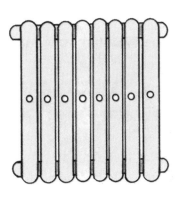

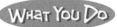
WHAT YOU DO

1. Mark the center of eight to 15 craft sticks (the more sticks, the larger your loom).

2. Drill a hole in the center of each stick. Use smaller drill bits for thinner sticks. Drill slowly and carefully to avoid cracking the wood; use a C-clamp or hold carefully with fingers.

3. Place two of the support pieces on the table to form the top and bottom of the loom. Space the drilled sticks evenly along the supports, leaving spaces between each drilled stick. Glue together.

4. Glue two more support sticks to the top and bottom of the loom. Let the glue harden completely. Decorate your loom with colored pens or pencils.

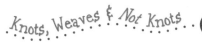

✳ Weave a Belt & Headband ✳

Now put that loom to use!

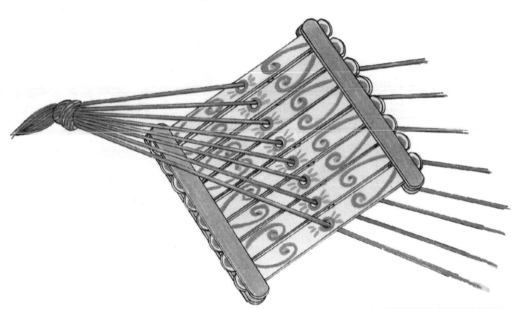

What You Need

* Yarn (many colors) 15 to 60 yards (13.5 to 54 m)
* Yard- or meter stick
* Scissors
* Paper clip
* A strong belt or rope to go around your waist

What You Do

SETTING UP THE WARP

1. Cut the yarn in 1 to 2 yard (1 to 2 m) lengths. Cut enough pieces so that you have one piece for each loom slit and one for each hole (for the loom shown here, you need 15 pieces).

2. Feed one strand of the same color yarn through each hole, using an opened paper clip to push the yarn through. When all the holes have a strand of yarn, tie the ends together loosely on each side of the loom.

3. Now, feed one strand of another color yarn through each slit.

4. Untangle all the ends and tie them together tightly, away from the loom. Now that you've set up the *warp*, or the lengthwise background for your weaving, you're ready to weave!

. . . *Incredibly Fun Crafts*

Warping Changes

When you put one color yarn through the holes and another color yarn through the slits, you get crosswise stripes. To get *lengthwise* stripes, put the same color yarn in the holes and slits that are next to each other. Hmmm. Using what you now know, can you figure out how to get a checkerboard pattern?

See how many ways you can change the pattern by changing how you warp the loom.

WEAVING!

1. Attach one knotted end of the yarn to your belt. Tie the other yarn end to a doorknob, table leg, or a nail pounded in a handy place. (In the mood to be silly? Tie the yarn to your toe!) Pull the yarn tight, so there's no slack.

2. Hold a small ball of yarn in one hand; then, pull the loom up with the other hand. The yarn in the slits will stay down while the yarn in the holes gets pulled up.

3. Pass the yarn ball through from left to right. Leave a few inches of the yarn end hanging out on the left side.

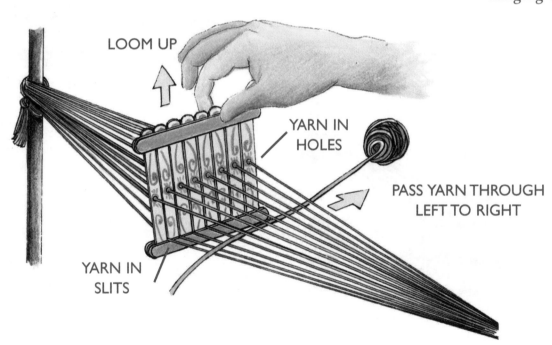

LOOM UP

YARN IN HOLES

PASS YARN THROUGH LEFT TO RIGHT

YARN IN SLITS

Warping answer: You could put red yarn in the first and second holes, yellow in the first and second slits. Then put blue in the next two holes, and green in the next two slits. Keep alternating red/yellow and blue/green until you run out of space on your loom. You'll get a checkerboard when you weave!

4. Now, push *down* on the loom with one hand; use the other hand to separate the yarn and to push the previous row snugly toward your waist. Then pass the ball of yarn through from right to left until the yarn is even with the right edge.

5. Pull the loom up again. Snug the previous row up to the first row. Pass the ball of yarn through from left to right again. Continue alternating up and down, weaving back and forth with the ball of yarn.

6. When you've woven as far as you can, untie the knot from the far end and pull the loom off the yarn. Untie it from your belt, trim the ends, and make small knots in the yarn ends.

Crafter's Clues

Roll On

When the woven part gets so long that you have to reach too far forward for comfort, roll the finished part up at your waist and move closer to the tied end.

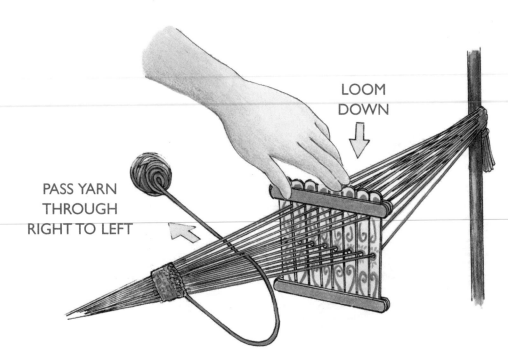

LOOM DOWN

PASS YARN THROUGH RIGHT TO LEFT

TAKING IT FURTHER

Weaving Changes

Can you figure out how to get only the *warp* (the lengthwise yarn) to show? Can you make both the warp and the *weft* (the widthwise yarn) show? Hint: It all depends on how tightly you pull the weft thread and how narrow you make the belt. Both ways make beautiful belts!

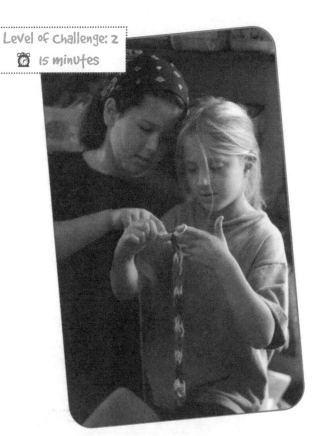

✳ Cat's-Tail Finger-Knitting ✳

Make lacy yarn out of a single strand. All you need for this easy knitting project is a ball of yarn and your fingers. Use your cat's-tail creation for a bookmark, a bracelet, a choker, a belt, or a fancy string tie. As you finger-knit, you'll be using the same technique that the first knitters in ancient Egypt and Peru used!

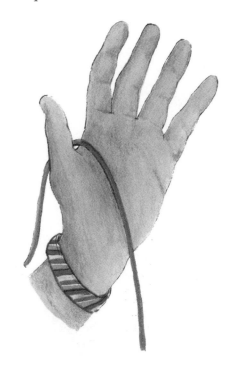

WHAT YOU DO

1. Let 6" (15 cm) of yarn dangle down the back of your hand between your thumb and index finger.

2. Wind the yarn over the index finger, under the next, over the ring finger, and under and around your pinkie finger.

3. Continue winding, going back under your ring finger, over your middle finger, and under and around your index finger. Repeat the whole sequence, index finger to pinkie and back again, once more.

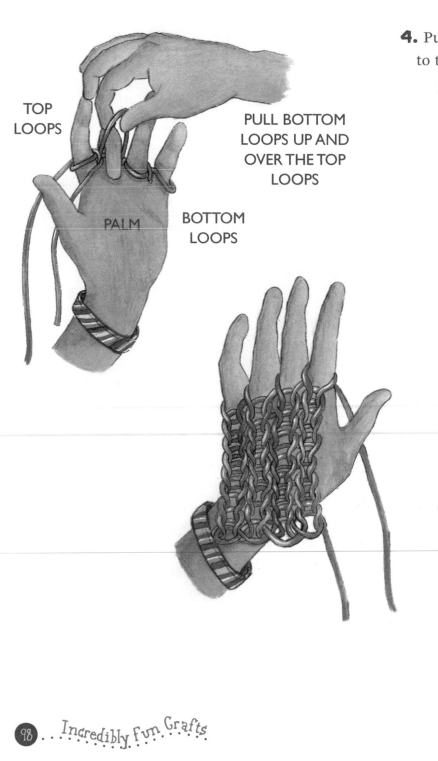

TOP LOOPS

PULL BOTTOM LOOPS UP AND OVER THE TOP LOOPS

PALM

BOTTOM LOOPS

4. Pull the bottom loop on each finger over the top loop (and off your finger to the back side of your hand). You have knitted one row.

5. Repeat the winding pattern down to your pinkie and back again one time to make the next new row of loops. Then loop each bottom loop on each finger over the new top loop to make another knitted row.

6. Continue finger-knitting the yarn, forming a "snake" trailing down the back of your hand. Pull down on the yarn dangling off the back of your hand to see how your knitting looks.

7. When you've knitted the length you want, cut off the extra yarn and slip the end through all the loops, so the yarn doesn't unravel.

INCREDIBLE CRAFTS FROM NATURE

There is something so refreshing about working with natural wild materials such as grasses and vines. The colors are quiet, the textures are real, and it just feels right to put nature's bounty to good use. Working with grasses and vines is fun (and inexpensive, too). Perhaps you'll put a homemade wreath on your bedroom or classroom door for all to enjoy. Or, make a vine basket and fill it with flowers or your favorite treasures. You can even craft wheat or straw into intricate-looking animals and shapes, Scandinavian style! Whatever you decide to create, you'll feel good because you're doing your part to save the earth. Start by looking around you — you'll find plenty of inspiration for expressing your individuality in nature!

Level of Challenge: 2
1 hour gathering and pruning
overnight soaking
2 to 3 hours assembly

✳ Wonderful Wreaths ✳

It's traditional to make circular wreaths at the time of the winter solstice (page 42) to represent the way the seasons go around and around forever. Make yours out of vines, fragrant evergreens, or pinecones, seeds, and other nature finds and decorate them however you like!

VINE WREATHS

The ancient Romans gave wreaths as gifts for the New Year to bring good luck — an old tradition that's fun to continue today, anytime of year. As the seasons change, you can change the wreath decorations. Nature always has something for you to feature!

What You Need

* Grapevines or other vines
* Garbage-bag twist ties (dark or green ones)

What You Do

1. Use freshly pruned vines or soak dry vines in water overnight in a large tub, bathtub, or clean garbage can.

2. Starting with the larger end of the vine, form a circle 16" to 18" (40 to 45 cm) in diameter. Tie it securely with a twist tie.

3. Wind the rest of the vine in and out around the circle until it's used up.

4. Add another vine, tucking it in where the first vine ended and adding a twist tie if needed. Wind it in and out around the circle.

5. Continue until you have gone around the wreath circle four to 10 times. With very thin vines you may need to go around as many as 20 times to make a strong wreath.

6. Let the wreath dry for about an hour; decorate (page 102).

Finding Nature's Bounty

People from many cultures gather natural materials to use in wreathmaking and basketmaking. Look around your backyard or neighborhood for materials to make a wreath or basket. Do you have any grapevines or other vines growing? Gather some (ask permission first!) and see if they're flexible. Weeds that wind themselves around trees also make good weaving material, because they are flexible — plus you are helping the tree. Ask a local gardener or landscaper to save vine prunings from the yards he or she works in, or call the Parks or Highway department for discarded trimmings. If no local vine prunings are available, you can buy materials from a craft or florist shop.

TAKING IT FURTHER

Rest on Your Laurels

Have you ever heard that expression? Early laurel wreaths were worn on the head to symbolize great achievements. (Laurel is a kind of tree.) In ancient Greece, wreaths made of laurel leaves were awarded for excellence in athletics and music. In ancient Rome, laurel wreaths were awarded as prizes for military achievements.

Make a wreath to crown yourself or a special person in your life. What trait or achievement are you most proud of?

Adding Pizzazz

Decorating Techniques

Use these basic decorating techniques to create a variety of wreaths.

* **Gift wreath.** Consider unusual decorations such as small boxes wrapped in pretty paper to look like "presents."

* **Nature's treasures.** Collect dry seedpods and berries from your yard, the park, or a fall garden. Save your nectarine, apricot, peach, and plum pits.

* **Flowery fun.** Use fresh flowers (watch them droop and dry and still be beautiful) or flowers dried with silica gel or very dry sand. To properly dry them, layer the flowers (roses and zinnias work well) carefully in the gel or sand so they don't touch each other. Cover the container tightly. Check the flowers in a few days. When dry, tie and glue them onto your wreath.

* **Recycled wreaths.** Use various recyclable materials such as yarn, beads, and red netting "bows" from fruit and vegetable bags. Attach ribbons and pretty papers from old presents, or make "flowers" out of plastic pull strips and colored plastic lids.

NATURE'S OWN

Make beautiful wreaths from natural "found" objects in your own backyard or favorite park. Anything goes here: Your wreath will be different than any others, decorated with whatever you collect!

What You Need

* Large and small plates or other flat, circular objects, for tracing
* Thick cardboard
* Sharp craft scissors, utility knife, or serrated knife*
* Glue or glue gun
* Branches, seedpods, nuts, pebbles, pinecones, and other interesting finds

   Use only with adult supervision

What You Do

1. Trace around the larger plate onto the cardboard. Cut out the circle.

2. Trace and cut out the smaller plate in the center of the larger cardboard circle.

3. Glue the natural objects onto the plain side of the cardboard. Cover the whole surface of the cardboard, gluing objects close together or even overlapping them.

4. Let the wreath dry completely; then, hang it on your door, over the mantle, or wherever pleases you!

 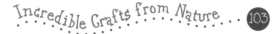

EVERGREEN WREATHS

Make a traditional wreath full of evergreen boughs that's individualized by your choice of decorations. It's easy to do — and so much better than store-bought!

Level of Challenge: 1
1 hour pruning (optional)
1 to 2 hours assembly

What You Need

* All-metal coat hanger
* Needle-nose pliers
* Evergreen boughs
* Vegetable-wrapping wires (from lettuce, spinach), with paper removed, or green garbage-bag twist ties

What You Do

1. Bend the coat hanger into a circle, using pliers as necessary. Leave the hook in place to hang the wreath later.

2. Tie evergreen boughs to the circle, using the ties to secure them in several places. You want your wreath to be thick and the wire completely covered.

3. Decorate as desired, and hang someplace special!

Level of Challenge: 3
1 hour gathering and pruning
overnight soaking
⏰ 2 hours Creating

✳ Very Fine Vine Basket ✳

Handmade baskets are unique — no two are exactly alike. People around the world make baskets in different sizes and shapes, depending on what plants grow where they live. Baskets differ also in how they're used — from gathering vegetables and flowers from the garden to holding groceries instead of using plastic or paper bags. Some are even so tightly woven that they hold water!

Make your baskets out of vines and other flexible plants that you can find around your neighborhood, and use them for whatever you like!

What You Need

* Grapevines or other thin, flexible, strong vines
* Yarn
* Weaving material (flat, flexible strips), such as thin vines, yarn, raffia, or grass or reeds about 15" (37.5 cm) long
* Clothespins
* Glue gun or glue

What You Do

MAKING THE FRAMEWORK

1. Select two strong vines that are 4' to 6' (1.2 to 2 m) long. If your vine isn't freshly pruned, you may need to soak it in water overnight to soften it.

2. Make a wreath from each vine by forming a circle about 20" (50 cm) around, tying it with the yarn, and winding the rest of the vine's length in and out around the circle (page 101).

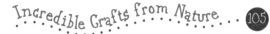

3. Tie the two wreaths at right angles to hold them in place temporarily. One wreath will become the rim of the basket, and the other will be the handle and the bottom of the basket.

4. To secure the two wreaths, use a God's eye corner (see GOD's EYE PRACTICE, page 107) at either side, where the wreaths cross. To start, tie a 1- to 2-yard (1 to 2 m) piece of yarn at one of the crosses where the two wreaths meet. Make a strong God's eye, using all the yarn. *Important:* The X where the vines cross should be held securely in place by the yarn! Tie the end of the yarn so it won't unravel. Then make a second God's eye at the other crossing.

5. Cut four or six vines to 10" (25 cm) lengths. Curve them so they're caught in the God's eyes at each side of the basket. These will form spokes for the basket bottom.

6. Glue the spokes securely into the yarn.

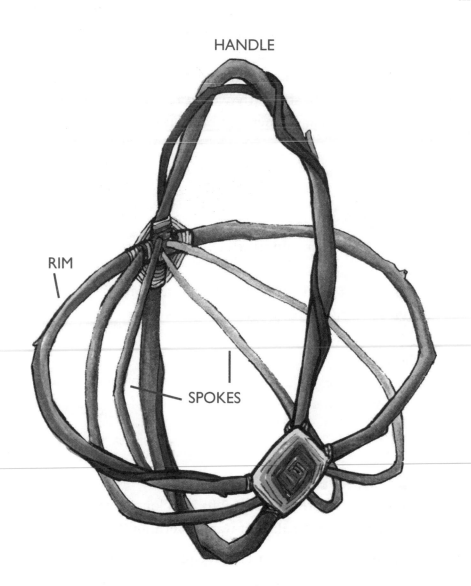

HANDLE

RIM

SPOKES

Cooking in Baskets

The native Californians didn't use clay for pottery; instead, they cooked in watertight woven baskets. But how, you might ask, was water boiled or food cooked in a vine basket without the basket burning? The coastal Miwok Indians solved the problem by heating rocks in the fire and then putting them in the water in the basket. They would stir constantly, cooking whatever was in the basket without ever burning the reeds or vines.

God's Eye Practice

These four-cornered weavings, called Ojo de Dios or God's Eyes, come from the Huichol (wee-chol) of Mexico. The sticks pointing in four directions represent earth, fire, water, and air. To make one, hold two craft or Popsicle sticks in an X shape or cross. Holding the yarn end at the back, wind the yarn around the first stick. Now take it over and around the next stick (which, pulled tight, makes a diagonal across the front); then, over and around the next one. For easy weaving, just rotate the cross one turn each time. Continue around and around, placing the new strand outside the old. To add more colors, just tie a new yarn to the end of the strand and keep weaving until you run out of yarn.

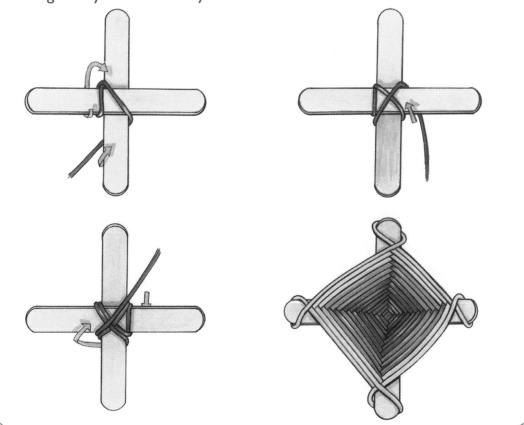

WEAVING THE BOTTOM

1. Now for some weaving fun! Weave with the long, flat, flexible strands to form the basket bottom. Starting at one rim, weave a strand in and out, in and out, from one rim to the other and back to the first rim.

2. When you use up one strand, start in with another.

3. Continue until the whole basket bottom is woven. Tuck the ends of each strand in and hold them with clothespins until the weaving materials have dried, then glue.

 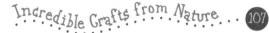

Level of challenge: 3
overnight soaking
⏰ ½ hour for each project

✳ Wheat Shapes ✳

A wreath, a heart, a star, a figure — even a goat! It's amazing what you can make with a few strands of straw or wheat! Try these shapes, then come up with your own.

What You Need

* Wheat or rye stalks with flowers, 12" (30 cm) long (available in craft stores) or tall, wild grasses
* Thin wire, yarn, or embroidery floss, cut to 3" (7.5 cm) lengths
* Ribbons
* Scissors

Heartfelt Harvests

For 9,000 years, wheat has been such an important food crop in Europe, Russia, the Middle East, and India that people give thanks with harvest rituals, some of which are still practiced today. Traditionally, people would gather some of the best or the last stalks of wheat from the harvest and make them into intricate shapes. The harvesters would gather around and sing a chant to the spirit of the wheat. In England, harvesters would then break into wonderful laughter and throw their caps in the air. A truly heartfelt celebration!

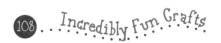

WHEAT WREATHS

What You Do

1. Soak the wheat or rye in lukewarm water overnight. Tie three wheat or wild grass stalks securely at the head (flower) end.

2. Braid the three stalks by putting the right stalk over the middle stalk; then, the left over the middle; then, the right over the middle; and the left over the middle, continuing the pattern (page 92) until you braid to the bottom.

3. Curve the braid around in a circle and tie it in place.

4. Cover the tie with a ribbon bow. Make a hook out of the wire to hang the wreath, if desired.

The Power of Tradition

On the first day of winter in Denmark, Sweden, and Norway, people used to tie wheat sheaves to the tops of tall poles to ward off evil spirits that they believed raced around on the cold, dark nights of winter — a tradition that may have been inspired by the sound of the howling winter winds. Today, many people continue the tradition of hanging wheat sheaves, but for a different purpose: to feed the hungry winter birds!

Let It Grow

If you let lawn grass grow, it gets tall and beautiful, and has pretty grass flowers. Some grasses have lacy, compact flowers; others have prickly seeds. But you can only see them if you let your grass grow!

Start a wild spot at the edge of your lawn or throw some wheat or rye seeds in an unclaimed patch of land to grow your own stalks.

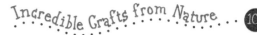

SCANDINAVIAN HEARTS

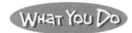

What You Do

1. Tie six wheat or wild grass stalks securely at the head (flower) end.

2. Tie the stalks again, about 2" (5 cm) down from the heads.

3. Divide the six stalks into two groups of three. Braid each group of three in a tight braid so you have two braids. Tie the ends of each braid with wire or yarn.

4. Curve the two braids around to form two halves of a heart. Attach them with wire or yarn behind the first tie.

5. Cover the tie with a ribbon bow. Attach a wire or an ornament hook, if desired. Then hang it up or give as a gift!

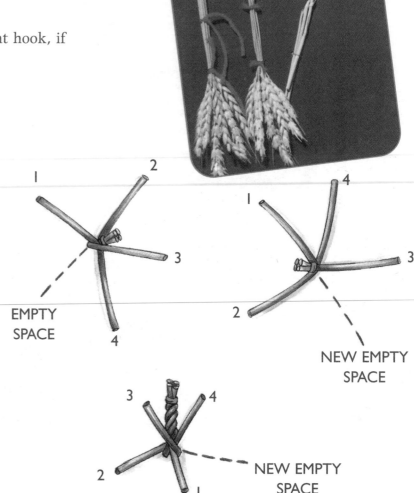

Special braids

If you like a challenge, you can use four stalks instead of the three called for in these weavings to give a 3-D effect. To make a wreath with the four stalks, spread out the stalks as spokes of a wheel, leaving space for an imaginary fifth stalk. Fold stalk 2 to the empty space and fold stalk 4 to the new space (where stalk 2 was). Now, fold stalk 1 to the new empty space and fold stalk 3 to the space where stalk 1 was. Repeat the pattern until the stalks are used up. Secure the ends of the braid with wire and twist to form the wreath.

To make a Scandinavian heart this way, start with eight grass stalks and divide them into two groups of four in step 3 (above).

EMPTY SPACE

NEW EMPTY SPACE

NEW EMPTY SPACE

STAR OF DAVID

To make this traditional Jewish shape, you first need to cut the flower heads off the wheat or wild grass stalks. Or, pull apart an old beach mat (ask permission first!) and use the individual stalks for your stars. The Star of David has six points formed by two overlapping triangular shapes.

What You Do

1. Gather twelve 10" (25 cm) stalks and divide into two piles of six. Cut 12 pieces of yarn to about 3" (7.5 cm).

2. Make a triangle out of the six stalks as shown. Tie the ends together with yarn, about 1" (2.5 cm) in from the ends. Repeat with the second pile.

3. Place one triangle on top of the other to form a six-pointed star. Tie them together where they intersect.

4. Add a yarn or wire hanger to hang your star.

WHEAT FIGURE

1. Cut six to 12 stalks to twice as long as you want your figure to be. Tie the bundle in the center with wire or yarn.

2. Fold the stalks in half and tie them where you want the neck to be.

3. Cut six to eight more stalks for arms. Lift up half of the tied stalks, separating the front and back stalks, and tuck the new stalks between them. Tie the waist.

4. Trim the arms to the desired shape and length. Tie the ends, if necessary. Attach a hook and hang, or add decorations, if desired.

Adding Pizzazz

Scrappy Duds

Dress up your wheat figure or angel in "real" clothes. Cut calico, lace, ribbon, and other fabric scraps into pants, shirts, and skirts; then, wrap, tie, or glue on the clothes.

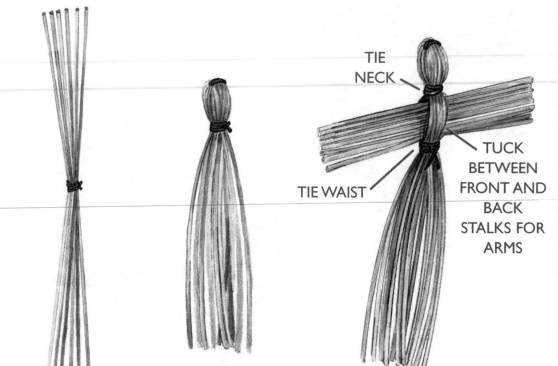

TIE NECK

TUCK BETWEEN FRONT AND BACK STALKS FOR ARMS

TIE WAIST

STRAW GOAT

In Finland and Norway, straw long-horned goats are made to go under the Christmas tree, a throwback to an earlier tradition where the goat was the pet of the Norse god Thor. At Christmastime, Scandinavian children still like to dress up as goats and be playful.

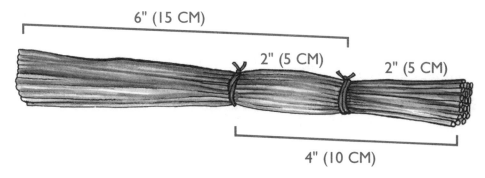

6" (15 CM)

2" (5 CM)

2" (5 CM)

4" (10 CM)

WHaT YoU Do

1. Cut 20 to 30 stalks about 8" (20 cm) long. Tie in a bunch with yarn at 2" (5 cm) and again at 4" (10 cm) from one end.

2. Bend down six stalks at the first tie for each rear leg and tie with yarn.

3. Braid the top three stalks into a tail and tie. Then, carefully cut off the rest of the stalks at the rear end.

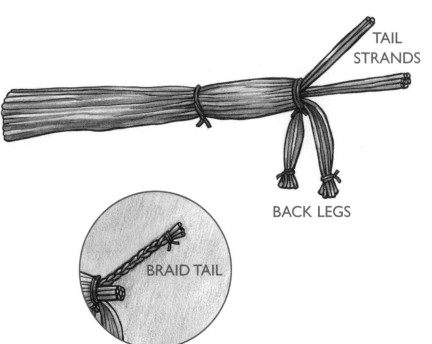

TAIL STRANDS

BACK LEGS

BRAID TAIL

4. Bend down six stalks at the second tie for each front leg. Trim 2" (5 cm) off the front legs; tie.

5. Slowly bend the remaining stalks up to form the neck, being careful not to break them. Tie at the head.

6. Braid two horns out of six stalks (three stalks for each horn).

7. Carefully bend down and tie the rest of the stalks to make the face and "goatee"!

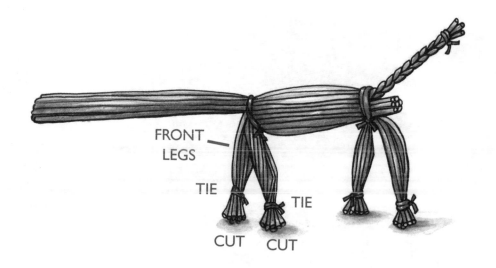

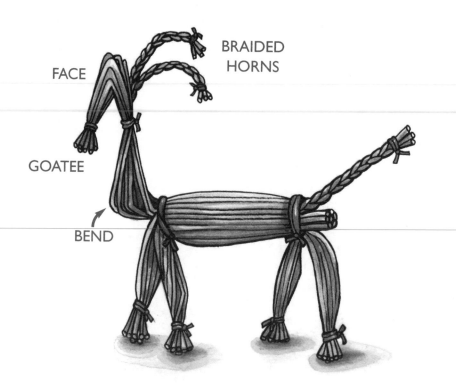

✳ Alter-Ego Scarecrows ✳

Everyone knows scarecrows are meant to protect crops from being harmed by birds, but did you know you can make them for plain old fun, too? Choose the traditional design to keep birds at bay, or create some stuffed friends that can sit on your front stoop or lounge around. You might even want a scarecrow look-alike to keep you company in your room!

TRADITIONAL SCARECROW

What You Need

* Old white, tan, or light brown sheet or pillowcase
* Scissors
* Straw (or wadded newspaper for indoor scarecrows)
* Twine, strong tape, glue gun, rubber bands, safety pins — whatever you have to hold it together
* Yarn
* Fabric paint and/or fine-tip permanent marker pens, all colors
* Old clothes, hats, gloves, accessories (including glasses, costume jewelry, neckties, scarves, belts, shoes, brooms, tools, etc.)
* Two straight sticks, 6' to 7' (1.75 to 2 m) long and 2' to 3' (.75 to 1 m) long
* Hammer (optional)

What You Do

MAKING THE HEAD

1. Cut a circle in the sheet about 1 yard (1 m) in diameter, and fill the center with straw. Gather the edges and tie at the neck. Or, use an old pillowcase, taking up the excess by taping or gluing a tuck in the back. (Pillowcases are so big that the head will look silly if you don't take a tuck.) Stuff with straw.

2. Glue on yarn hair. Paint or draw a face on the front of the head; let dry.

ASSEMBLING YOUR SCARECROW

1. Put one pant leg on the long stick; stuff both legs with straw.

2. Tie the short stick at right angles to the long stick, using twine or strong tape. Leave enough of the stick above the "shoulders" to attach the head.

3. Put one shirtsleeve on each end of the short stick.

4. Stuff the shirt with straw and pin or glue the shirt to the pants in several places. Leave the straw as hands, or stuff some gloves and pin them to the shirt wrists. Or, make hands or feet by drawing fingers or toes on stuffed white socks. Paint colorful patches on the shirt and pants, if you like; let dry.

5. Hammer the long post into the ground or set in place. Attach the head over the top of the stick, tucking the neck into the shirt. Add a hat, glasses, and any other accessories.

 Crafter's Clues

Stuff It!

◆ Use rubber bands to hold the wrists and ankles closed so the straw doesn't fall out while you're stuffing the body.

◆ To make a scarecrow in a dress, stuff tights or pajama bottoms to form legs, use a long-sleeved T-shirt or pajama top to form arms, and then put the dress over them.

◆ To fill socks with straw, turn the socks inside out. With your hand inside the sock, tightly grab a handful of straw. With the other hand, peel the sock off your arm, over the handful of straw.

Scare Some Crows!

* Dress your scarecrow in big billowy clothes and scarves so the wind makes them flap.

* Attach aluminum pie pans to the arms and legs so the wind makes your scarecrow clatter and reflect light.

* Attach strings and netting from the scarecrow to the ground and trees so there's a bird-frightening tangle.

Guardians of the Fields

Scarecrows have been around a long time — as long as 2,500 years! — ever since people began growing crops that needed to be protected. Ancient Greeks carved scarecrows from wood and gave them ugly, twisted-looking faces. Early Japanese scarecrows held a bow and arrow to make them look scary, while other scarecrows were made of fish bones and rags set afire. Early European farmers made witch-like scarecrows. In Nepal, farmers wove dog shapes out of split bamboo, which guarded fields of corn growing at 10,000 feet (3000 m) above sea level.

SOFT-SCULPTURE SCARECROW

You don't need to make your scarecrow stand up — you can make a big soft sculpture instead, using the same materials as for the traditional scarecrow, but without the sticks. Your soft, cushy friend probably won't work in a cornfield like a traditional scarecrow, but if you have it sitting on your front stoop — or lounging in a backyard tree — you'll certainly surprise the neighbors!

WHAT YOU DO

Stuff the head and clothes with straw (or newspaper for an indoor scarecrow). Use safety pins to attach pants to shirts, head to shirt neck, pajama tops to pajama bottoms, and so on. Put dresses or skirts over the stuffed clothes, if you wish. Add hats, belts, neckties, gloves, jewelry, and glasses. Then mold and shape your scarecrow's arms and legs to create the character and pose you want — sitting in a chair by the front door, lounging on the porch swing, or hanging out in your room!

New Life for Leftovers

Here are a few ideas for using your remaining straw:

✳ Have straw fights.

✳ Build straw forts and burrow into straw piles.

✳ Read *On the Banks of Plum Creek* by Laura Ingalls Wilder about sliding down straw stacks; then, jump into one yourself!

✳ When the straw starts to rot, use it as mulch for your garden or throw it on the compost pile!

BORING STUFF FOR ADULTS

YES! ADULTS MAY PARTICIPATE

I hope adults will be so captivated by these projects they'll say, "Pass the scissors, I'm making one, too!" When you join kids in doing these activities, you give them a chance to see adults who like to have fun and try new things.

For most of the projects, there should be time for the adults to enjoy crafting with the kids. If you like the craft project, any difficulties figuring out how to do it will be much easier to solve. When kids ask you questions, you don't have to know all the answers. You can wonder with them and work together to find the solutions!

Kids want to dive in; they're excited and full of ideas. Give encouragement and enjoy what they do. Help to set up the environment so it is safe (page 11) and help keep it positive with lots of encouragement. Be available to help solve design problems or to add an extra pair of hands when needed. But avoid directing the projects too much or defining how they should be done. Instead, let kids find their way with some minor direction from

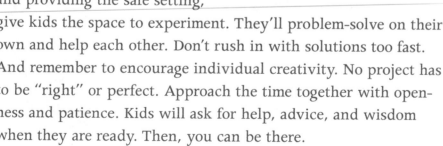

you. Allow them to learn from their mistakes and reinvent things. When kids ask for help, give them only the help they need at the moment, and then let them go at it again. They'll remember what they learned better this way.

After supplying the tools and providing the safe setting, give kids the space to experiment. They'll problem-solve on their own and help each other. Don't rush in with solutions too fast. And remember to encourage individual creativity. No project has to be "right" or perfect. Approach the time together with openness and patience. Kids will ask for help, advice, and wisdom when they are ready. Then, you can be there.

✳ What These Experiences Offer Kids ✳

✳ **FUN.** Kids will have fun doing these projects. Real education is joyful, a celebration of creative thought. Each child has a claim to fame. These projects help them find their unique contribution to the world.

✳ **MASTERY AND SELF-ESTEEM.** These activities give children a sense of mastery. If we try a lot of new things with kids, they can learn that they don't have to be experts to do things they've never done before, and they don't need an "expert" to do it for them. It gives them a sense of widening possibilities rather than feeling restricted and fearful in our modern world.

✳ **CONTROL.** If kids are given more control over their lives and surroundings, they will contribute more and take better care of their environment.

✳ **VARIETY.** Kids get a chance to use a lot of unusual materials in unique ways. Children are naturally inventive, and a variety of materials encourages individual thinking.

✳ **BEAUTY.** Much of what kids create is beautiful — not perfect, but beautiful in its idiosyncracies.

✳ **ACTIVE OBSERVATION.** Kids learn to actively observe in our world. By being involved in doing, kids become more alert and observe more closely. When kids are not being "taught at," but instead are "discovering with," they become their most intelligent selves.

✳ **INTEGRATED CURRICULUM.** Kids discover how every bit of learning ties to other bits of learning. From each activity, they can branch out into many intellectual disciplines if they so choose.

✳ **SAVE THE EARTH.** When we make things out of what we find, we can see where things come from and how they recycle themselves. By being frugal without being miserly, kids get maximum enjoyment out of minimal materials. This discovery in itself is exciting!

✳ **CULTURE.** Kids will draw on a variety of cultural roots, enjoying the "old ways" and valuing our different histories. Respect for others is a natural outgrowth of the shared experience of making art.

✳ **ENJOY UPREDICTABLE EXUBERANCE!** As you work with kids, try to let go of control and allow wildness. It's really more fun. Let your house be lived in, share your garden with animals. That doesn't mean you should abandon all housecleaning and ignore the garden, but allow for creative messes indoors and natural processes outdoors. Your kids will appreciate it!

INDEX

✳ About the Author ✳

Since 1990, Roberta Gould has organized and run an after-school and summer arts and adventure program for kids called "Amusing Muses" in California. She encourages kids to tap into their own creativity and joyful exuberance, creating with what they have on hand and exploring the crafts and traditions of people the world over.

Roberta has traveled extensively on a small budget in Asia, Mexico, and Europe. She has camped throughout Japan, on porches in Nepal, and on rooftops in India. It is on these trips that her love of varied cultures has gained the depth and breadth that she shares in her teaching and writing.

She once sailed in a small sailboat to Alaska, where she swam with seals, rowed among icebergs, ice skated on a glacial lake, climbed up mossy waterfalls, and saw a tree filled with eagles. She has kept goats, milked cows, watched her bees swarm, and found her "missing" hen when it appeared with 13 baby chicks.

As a joint project of the Alaska Native Brotherhood and the Alaska State Museum, Roberta designed and taught a cultural education program for children in Juneau, Alaska. There, she learned traditional skills from the elders and taught them to the young.

Roberta loves to folk dance, contra dance, and sing. She has sung with the San Francisco Symphony Chorus, the Oakland Symphony Chorus, and her family. She has taught rounds to elementary school students and has shared rounds with her friends and acquaintances all over the world. Recently, she performed in her 12th opera with the Berkeley Opera Chorus, including singing from the top of a ladder!

MORE GOOD BOOKS FROM WILLIAMSON PUBLISHING

Williamson books are available from your bookseller or directly from Williamson Publishing.
Please see last page for ordering information or to visit our website. Thank you.

Also by Roberta Gould!

THE MULTICULTURAL KIDS' CRAFT BOOK
50 Creative Activities from 30 Countries
A Williamson Multicultural *Kids Can!*® Book
Ages 8 to 14, 128 pages, **full-color** illustrations and photographs, trade paper, 11 x 8½, $14.95 US/$23.95 CAN

Williamson's *Kids Can!*® Books ...
The following *Kids Can!*® books for ages 7 to 14 are 128 to 176 pages, fully illustrated, trade paper, 11 x 8½, $12.95 US/$19.95 CAN.

Art & Crafts

Parents' Choice Recommended
ForeWord Magazine Book of the Year Finalist
PAPER-FOLDING FUN!
50 Awesome Crafts to Weave, Twist & Curl
by Ginger Johnson

Parents' Choice Recommended
The Kids' Guide to MAKING SCRAPBOOKS & PHOTO ALBUMS!
How to Collect, Design, Assemble, Decorate
by Laura Check

JAZZY JEWELRY
Power Beads, Crystals, Chokers, & Illusion and Tattoo Styles
by Diane Baker

American Bookseller Pick of the Lists
Dr. Toy Best Vacation Product
KIDS' CRAZY ART CONCOCTIONS
50 Mysterious Mixtures for Art & Craft Fun
by Jill Frankel Hauser

Parents' Choice Gold Award
American Bookseller Pick of the Lists
THE KIDS' MULTICULTURAL ART BOOK
Art & Craft Experiences from Around the World
by Alexandra M. Terzian

Parents' Choice Recommended
Orbus Pictus Award for Outstanding Nonfiction
KIDS' ART WORKS!
Creating with Color, Design, Texture & More
by Sandi Henry
Teachers' Choice Award
Dr. Toy Best Vacation Product

CUT-PAPER PLAY!
Dazzling Creations from Construction Paper
by Sandi Henry

American Bookseller Pick of the Lists
Parents' Choice Recommended
ADVENTURES IN ART
Arts & Crafts Experiences for 8- to 13-Year Olds
by Susan Milord

Parents' Choice Approved
KIDS CREATE!
Art & Craft Experiences for 3- to 9-Year-Olds
by Laurie Carlson

American Bookseller Pick of the Lists
Skipping Stones Nature & Ecology Honor Award
EcoArt!
Earth-Friendly Art & Craft Experiences for 3- to 9-Year-Olds
by Laurie Carlson

Benjamin Franklin Best Education/Teaching Book Award
Parent's Guide Children's Media Award
HAND-PRINT ANIMAL ART
by Carolyn Carreiro
full-color, $14.95

Early Childhood News Directors' Choice Award
Real Life Award
VROOM! VROOM!
Making 'dozers, 'copters, trucks & more
by Judy Press

Williamson's *Kids Can!*® Books

SCIENCE & MATH

Around-the-Globe MATH ADVENTURES
Amazing Activities to Explore Math's Multicultural Roots!
by Ann McCallum
full-color, $14.95

FIZZ, BUBBLE & FLASH!
Element Explorations & Atom Adventures for Hands-On Science Fun!
by Anita Brandolini, Ph.D.

Parents' Choice Silver Honor Award
Awesome OCEAN SCIENCE!
Investigating the Secrets of the Underwater World
by Cindy A. Littlefield

Parents' Choice Recommended
Children's Digest Health Education Award
The Kids' Guide to FIRST AID
All about Bruises, Burns, Stings, Sprains & Other Ouches
by Karen Buhler Gale, R.N.

REAL-WORLD MATH for Hands-On Fun!
by Cindy A. Littlefield

Parents' Choice Recommended
THE KIDS' BOOK OF WEATHER FORECASTING
Build a Weather Station, "Read" the Sky & Make Predictions!
with meteorologist Mark Breen and Kathleen Friestad

Parents' Choice Honor Award
THE KIDS' NATURAL HISTORY BOOK
Making Dinos, Fossils, Mammoths & More
by Judy Press

Parents' Choice Honor Award
American Institute of Physics Science Writing Award
GIZMOS & GADGETS
Creating Science Contraptions that Work (& Knowing Why)
by Jill Frankel Hauser

American Bookseller Pick of the Lists
Benjamin Franklin Best Juvenile Nonfiction Award
SUPER SCIENCE CONCOCTIONS
50 Mysterious Mixtures for Fabulous Fun
by Jill Frankel Hauser

American Bookseller Pick of the Lists
Oppenheim Toy Portfolio Best Book Award
THE KIDS' SCIENCE BOOK
Creative Experiences for Hands-On Fun
by Robert Hirschfeld and Nancy White

Parents' Choice Gold Award
Dr. Toy Best Vacation Product
THE KIDS' NATURE BOOK
365 Indoor/Outdoor Activities & Experiences
by Susan Milord

THE KIDS' WILDLIFE BOOK
Exploring Animal Worlds through Indoor/Outdoor Experiences
by Warner Shedd

Williamson's *Kids Can!*® Books
CREATIVE, ACTIVE FUN

KIDS MAKE MAGIC!
The Complete Guide to Becoming an Amazing Magician
by Ron Burgess

GREAT GAMES!
Ball, Board, Quiz & Word, Indoors & Out, for Many or Few!
by Sam Taggar

American Bookseller Pick of the Lists
Parents' Choice Approved
SUMMER FUN!
60 Activities for a Kid-Perfect Summer
by Susan Williamson

Selection of Book-of-the-Month; Scholastic Book Clubs
KIDS COOK!
Fabulous Food for the Whole Family
by Sarah Williamson and Zachary Williamson

Parents' Choice Approved
Benjamin Franklin Best Multicultural Book Award
THE KIDS' MULTICULTURAL COOKBOOK
Food & Fun Around the World
by Deanna F. Cook

Parents' Choice Approved
Parent's Guide Children's Media Award
BOREDOM BUSTERS!
The Curious Kids' Activity Book
by Avery Hart and Paul Mantell

Parents' Choice Gold Award
Benjamin Franklin Best Juvenile Nonfiction Award
KIDS MAKE MUSIC!
Clapping and Tapping from Bach to Rock
by Avery Hart and Paul Mantell

HANDS AROUND THE WORLD
365 Creative Ways to Build Cultural Awareness & Global Respect
by Susan Milord

Parents' Choice Approved
Dr. Toy Best Vacation Product
KIDS GARDEN!
The Anytime, Anyplace Guide to Sowing & Growing Fun
by Avery Hart and Paul Mantell

Parents Magazine Parents' Pick
Real Life Award
KIDS LEARN AMERICA!
Bringing Geography to Life with People, Places & History
by Patricia Gordon and Reed C. Snow

Williamson's *Quick Starts for Kids!*® Books …
Quick Starts for Kids!® books for children, ages 8 and older, are each 64 pages, fully illustrated, trade paper, 8½ x 11, $8.95 US/$10.95 CAN.

CREATE A YEAR-ROUND WILDLIFE HABITAT
For Urban & Suburban Small Spaces
by Robyn Haus

MAKE YOUR OWN COOL CARDS
40 Awesome Notes & Invitations!
by Peg Blanchette & Terri Thibault

ALMOST-INSTANT SCRAPBOOKS
by Laura Check

KIDS' EASY BIKE CARE
Tune-Ups, Tools & Quick Fixes
by Steve Cole

ForeWord Magazine Book of the Year Finalist
DRAWING HORSES
(that look real!)
by Don Mayne

MAKE YOUR OWN CHRISTMAS ORNAMENTS
by Ginger Johnson

Really Cool FELT CRAFTS
by Peg Blanchette and Terri Thibault

GARDEN FUN!
Indoors & Out; In Pots & Small Spots
by Vicky Congdon

40 KNOTS TO KNOW
Hitches, Loops, Bends & Bindings
by Emily Stetson

MAKE YOUR OWN FUN PICTURE FRAMES!
by Matt Phillips

MAKE YOUR OWN HAIRWEAR
Beaded Barrettes, Clips, Dangles & Headbands
by Diane Baker

Parents' Choice Approved
BAKE THE BEST-EVER COOKIES!
by Sarah A. Williamson

BE A CLOWN!
Techniques from a Real Clown
by Ron Burgess

Dr. Toy 100 Best Children's Books
Dr. Toy 10 Best Socially Responsible Books
MAKE YOUR OWN BIRDHOUSES & FEEDERS
by Robyn Haus

YO-YO!
Tips & Tricks from a Pro
by Ron Burgess

Oppenheim Toy Portfolio Gold Award
DRAW YOUR OWN CARTOONS!
by Don Mayne

KIDS' EASY KNITTING PROJECTS
by Peg Blanchette

KIDS' EASY QUILTING PROJECTS
by Terri Thibault

American Bookseller Pick of the Lists
MAKE YOUR OWN TEDDY BEARS & BEAR CLOTHES
by Sue Mahren

Visit Our Website! • • • • • • • • • • •
To see what's new at Williamson and learn more about specific books, visit our website at: **www.williamsonbooks.com**

WIN a gift certificate!
New winner every month!

Be a Williamson *You Can Do It!*™ Winner!

SEND IN YOUR PROJECT PHOTOS AND WRITINGS TO ENTER!
NOW you can see selected projects from readers just like you posted on our website! And one project per month will be named a *You Can Do It!*™ winner. The winning child, family, or group will receive a gift certificate for Williamson Books (that the winner can select)!

Visit our website to see how to enter the Williamson *You Can Do It!*™ **contest. Once you enter, visit our website to see if your project is posted and to see if you are a Williamson Winner:** www.williamsonbooks.com.

Free Teacher's Guide!
If you are a schoolteacher or are homeschooling your family, please visit our website <www.williamsonbooks.com> and click on "For Teachers, Parents & Caregivers" to download a FREE Teacher's Guide with additional classroom ideas, activities, and projects.

128

To Order Books:

You'll find Williamson books wherever high-quality children's books are sold, or order directly from Williamson Publishing.

Toll-free phone orders with credit cards:
1-800-234-8791

We accept Visa and MasterCard
(please include the number and expiration date).

Or, send a check with your order to:
Williamson Publishing Company
P.O. Box 185
Charlotte, Vermont 05445

For a free catalog: mail, phone, or e-mail <info@williamsonbooks.com>

Please add **$4.00** for postage for one book plus **$1.00** for each additional book. Satisfaction is guaranteed or full refund without questions or quibbles.

Kids Can!®, *Little Hands*®, *Kaleidoscope Kids*®, *Quick Starts for Kids!*®, and *Tales Alive!*® are registered trademarks of Williamson Publishing.

Good Times™ and *You Can Do It!*™ are trademarks of Williamson Publishing.